Seeing

Behind

the

Masks

A book about

Seeing

being real,

Behind

being loving,

the

being transparent.

Masks

JIM TOOMBS

MULTNOMAH BOOKS

SEEING BEHIND THE MASKS
published by Multnomah Books
a part of the Questar publishing family

© 1995 by Jim Toombs

International Standard Book Number: 0-88070-676-7

Cover photo by Larry Bercow

Cover design by David Carlson

Printed in the United States of America

Scripture quotations are from:
The Holy Bible, New International Version (NIV)
© 1973, 1984 by International Bible Society,
used by permission of Zondervan Publishing House

For information:
QUESTAR PUBLISHERS, INC.
POST OFFICE BOX 1720
SISTERS, OREGON 97759

95 96 97 98 99 00 01 02 — 10 9 8 7 6 5 4 3 2 1

To Tammy, Rachel, Michael, and Geoffrey.

You are each unique gifts from God.

CONTENTS

ACKNOWLEDGMENTS

While the author is responsible for everything written in a book, no book could be written without the input and support of other people. I am especially fortunate at the Oak Hills Church of Christ to be surrounded by gifted, wise, and talented people.

Charles Prince has been a friend for over twenty years, my "father in the faith." We on the staff lovingly refer to him as our "walking encyclopedia." Whenever there is a question on virtually any subject, Charles is a good source to consider. He is also a theological plumb bob in love with the Bible, in love with Jesus.

Glen Carter first introduced me to the idea that forgiving yourself is unbiblical. Pat Hile was kind enough to give me the benefit of his Doctor of Ministry course work without forcing me to actually travel to the bowels of West Texas to go to school with him. Vicki Williams has helped with her deep insights into human nature.

Max Lucado is a constant encouragement. Writing is fun and exciting and rewarding. It is also arduous, lonely work. Sometimes it can be deeply frustrating. Max has experienced all of that, and he has been kind enough to share his experiences with me at critical moments. He's also a great cheerleader, a constant encourager.

I also must thank each and every member of the Oak Hills Singles Ministry. They have stood by me through this entire process. Sometimes, at key times, they have had to do without me. And they did just fine.

And thank you, Jesus, for your constant presence. There are many truths about you that encourage me. But that all authority in heaven and on earth has been given to you is often what keeps me going. No matter how difficult the struggles, no matter how aggressive the Accuser gets, he is no match for you. Your power, your glory, your grace are supreme. I look forward to your return.

Walls

Welcome to my childhood garden.
Come in and smell the roses.
The walls are low, the thorns are few,
the grass still damp from the morning dew.

There are no fears, not even tears,
then winter brings the frost.
And the garden dies as the lone child cries
and all but solitude is lost.

The walls grow higher around the crier,
enshrouding him in shadow.
They shield from pain, but block the rain,
that makes the flowers grow.

Welcome to my secret garden.
I wish you could come in.
The child's inside where he'll always hide
until the Light comes shining through.

Chapter 1

The Mask Falls

"Carry each other's burdens, and in this way you will fulfill the law of Christ." Galatians 6:2

It was Sunday morning, December 9, 1973.

1973—not a year I would want to revisit. Though before that morning no one would have guessed what a hideous year it had been for me. My folks didn't know. My boss didn't know. Neither did the church. Not even my weekly Bible study group that had been meeting for the two years we had been in San Antonio.

No one knew. No one except perhaps my wife. And she didn't care.

So far as the world could tell, my life was clicking along just fine. The face I presented on every front was utter normality. We were a happy, young Christian family.

"How's the job, Jim?"

"Fine, thanks." Smile.

"Wife doing OK?"

"Sure. Everything's fine." Friendly nod of the head.

"How about those two girls?"

"No problem." Hands open, palms up, in a gesture of honesty.

They were lies, every one of them. How could I say such things? The job was going well, except I wasn't making enough money to support my family. Nor was I apt to. And my wife was not doing well. She was trapped in a web of sin she was either unable or unwilling to break out of. Our family was in shambles and had been ever since she told me she no longer loved me.

But how could I tell anyone that? How could I admit I had lost control of my family and my life? How could I reveal the real me—the broken, scared, bewildered, and angry young man behind the smile? I needed help, but I was too afraid of what might happen—the rejection, the judgment, the gossip—to say anything to anyone.

I had been a Christian for just under four years. Coming to Christ had been hard for me. First of all I wanted to make sure Christianity was intellectually respectable before I got on board. Secondly I had a distorted notion of God. For me he was a stern parent who was waiting for me to make a mistake so he could gleefully whack me.

Jesus was just part of the setup. Become a Christian, be like Jesus, be saved…and mess up as everyone does sooner or later. Then get punished for not being perfect. I couldn't be like Jesus. He was an unattainable ideal. He was perfect. And while I wanted to be perfect, I knew it for a fool's dream. So if I'm doomed to fail before I start, why try? If I took this gambit, God would be whacking me until the cows came home and laughing through his teeth that he had suckered me so well.

No, becoming a Christian hadn't been an easy decision for me.

Learning to trust wasn't either. After I became a Christian, I knew God would get to know me. I mean *really* get to know me. And I was afraid that when he got to know me he wouldn't like what he knew. Perhaps the same thoughts about the church were going through my head during 1973 when my life was crumbling. Here I was, dying inside yet hiding my pain from the people who had become closer than some of my family. I couldn't let them see for fear they would turn from me and against me once they knew my failures.

The problem, though, was the Bible. I was reading it for the first time in my life, and it kept speaking to me. "You have not because you ask not." "Bear one another's burdens." "By this they will know you are my disciples, if you love one another." "God is love." There was so much hope in those phrases. There was hope that I was wrong, that God really did love me and so did his church.

If one of the jobs of Christ's church was to intercede for each other, how could my fellow Christians intercede for me when they didn't know I was in pain? How could they love me if they didn't know who I really was? How could they bear my burdens if they never knew I was carrying any?

But I kept them away. My smile became more brittle. My eyes took on a haunted look behind the plastic facade. Yet only the most perceptive had a clue anything was wrong. And when they asked, I tightened the smile one more notch and "just fine-d" them.

Until Sunday morning, December 9.

I don't remember what Charles Prince, the preacher, was saying that morning. I doubt I was really listening because I had my own spiritual agenda. I was swinging in tighter and tighter emotional arcs now. I couldn't keep the secret much longer. I felt as if I would explode. Yet, it wasn't just my secret. It was my wife's too. Could I tell of my pain without exposing her? Would telling everyone affect our chances of reconciling? And what about my part in our problems? Could I bear the pain of exposure? Could I bear the shame? Could I wait another minute?

My heart was sick to death. My soul was bleeding. I was desperate. I was ashamed of both the state of my marriage and my lack of faith in God's promises and his church.

These were my friends, my family. God had said to call on them in times of need, and boy was this a time of need! I needed help. I needed prayer. No one could "do" anything, but they could pray for us—but only if they knew.

At last I made a decision. When Charles issued the invitation for prayers, I got up from my pew and shuffled forward with a dry mouth and trembling legs. It was the first time I had come forward since the day I was baptized in 1970.

"Charles, I need to ask for prayers. I'd like to address the congregation."

"All right, Jim. Just let me tell them what you want to do."

As the final notes of the song died down, Joe Cannon, the song leader, stepped off the platform, and Charles took his place behind the microphone. "Our brother Jim Toombs has come forward with a special prayer request he wants to share with you. Jim," he said, extending his hand to me.

My memory of those moments is vague and sketchy, more impressions than details. I remember saying something like, "The Bible says if you have a problem you should share it with your brothers and sisters and get them to pray for you. The problem I have is a big one, but it's not just mine. It's my wife's, too. We're having an awful time right now. There are some real serious problems in our marriage...and I'm afraid we're not going to make it." Tears filled my eyes, and I struggled to keep my voice from catching. "We need your prayers. Will you pray with me?"

The auditorium was still and quiet as people bowed their heads.

"Father, you know what's been going on. You know how hard things have been. You know what needs to happen. I pray that you will please do something soon. God, thank you for these people, your church. Please hear my prayers."

As I turned to step away from the microphone, a giant blur grabbed me in a huge bear hug. It was Joe Cannon. Joe was the quarterback on our sandlot, Sunday afternoon football team, but he was built more like a tackle. A big tackle. He was weeping as he engulfed my hundred and twenty-five pounds in his big arms. I'll never forget that moment. It was the perfect, God-ordained thing for Joe to do. It was what I needed. He just held me and told me he loved me and cried for me. It was almost more than I could bear as I fought both the urge to run and the urge to wail.

And Joe wasn't the only one. He was just the first. Others came up to express their love and concern—elders, their wives, men and women from our Bible study, and some I didn't know at all. All wanted to let me know that they hurt with me. No one told me I was bad. No one told me to find another church. No one gave me the impression I would be shunned the following Sunday.

And I wasn't. Nothing of what I had most feared came to pass as I looked out from behind my mask that Sunday morning.

WHY DO WE WEAR MASKS?

We certainly don't wear masks because they are light and easy to bear. Anything but!

Most often I think we wear masks because we're afraid to show others who we truly are. If they really knew us, they might not like us. They might reject us. We wouldn't be friends. We wouldn't be brothers. That's a lonely thought, the stuff of nightmares.

Fear is the most common emotion hidden behind the mask. We fear what others will think of us, how they will act towards us. Maybe they won't admire us if they see all this fear. Maybe they won't respect us if they find out how inadequate we feel. Maybe they will see we're not really very good Christians, especially compared to the preacher or the elders or Billy Graham. Or to them.

Or maybe the nameless, faceless, all powerful THEY will see that because of what we think and feel and the way we behave sometimes, we really don't have much value as human beings. They'll find we aren't worthwhile additions to the Kingdom. Then we will feel shame.

Shame—that horrible, debilitating emotion. The emotion that makes us want to crawl under the rug or hide behind the chair. Shame is the sense of humiliation we feel in dreams where we are the only ones in our underwear, naked and exposed to a world clothed in suits and pretty dresses. Shame is a feeling of discomfort with who we are more than the things we've done.

Our shame makes us fear we won't measure up, that we won't be the kind of Christian they think we should be. We're not even the kind of Christian we think we should be. Oh, they may believe we are holy and godly, but that is just the mask. If they really knew what we are like, they would want to go to another church. If Jesus knew what we are really like, he would want to go to another church. That's shame.

Or perhaps they will see we harbor a simmering pot of anger. It could be about the way we've been treated by our parents. Or our bosses. Or our mates. Or our children. Old flames. Old teachers. Or them.

Maybe they will see we have rage that even we are afraid to acknowledge, and they will be frightened to be around us. Maybe they'll see we are angry with God since he is the only one with the power to stop our pain and heal the losses, and we don't think he has done enough, fast enough, to help us.

We know God's forgiveness is a wonderful thing. We've read about it, but we may never have let ourselves experience it. So we fear if we ever let anyone see what is behind the masks we wear, not even God could forgive us. We are too sin-stained. Too weak. Too broken.

Most of us have a secret darkness in our souls we can never allow anyone to see. And so we continue on like Greek actors, *hupokrites*, whose real personae are nothing like the actors' masks they present on stage. And we are always on stage.

Don't you, like me, get tired of holding up the mask, so tired of pretending to be someone you're not? Doesn't it get heavy?

Will we ever be able to drop our charade? Will we ever be able to lay aside our masks this side of the grave? The thought of being free of such a burden is both exhilarating and terrifying. Because the mask that isolates also protects.

THE SIN OF SELF-PROTECTION

In his book *Inside Out* Larry Crabb says one of the greater sins we do our best to ignore is the sin of self-protection. It is the core sin, the sin within a sin. It is a sin for Christians because when we protect ourselves, when we hide behind our masks from those God has commanded us to love, we can't do what he has told us to do. Not only can we not truly love others, but we are not allowing them to love us either. We are not allowing ourselves to truly be involved and integrated into the church. The body of Christ only gets to see the part of us we want it to see. We show what we think are the good parts and hide all the bad parts.

Hiding is not loving. Hiding precludes loving. Our masks keep us from risking love for our neighbors. So our own ministry stops pretty much at the boundaries of our masks. No one gets in. And no one gets out.

Until the masks fall.

LIFTING THE MASK

1. Have you experienced such compassion as Joe Cannon demonstrated? Under what circumstances? What was the result?

2. James says if anyone is sick he should call the elders to pray over him (James 5:2). How can that scripture apply to a decision to seek help from the church? How might this scripture apply to those who seek the prayers of the church? What can happen to people who don't share their needs with their church family?

3. To what extent is it important for people seeking the prayers of the church to reveal the details of their problem? When is it better to seek the prayers of the entire church or a smaller group within the church?

4. What fears keep you from being transparent with your brothers and sisters? What is the source of those fears?

5. What have you needed to tell your church family but were unable to because of fear or anxiety? Have you ever been able to let down your mask? With whom? What was the result? What does it cost you to keep your mask in place?

Chapter 2

When God Was in Need

"He took Peter and the two sons of Zebedee along with him, and he began to be sorrowful and troubled. Then he said to them, 'My soul is overwhelmed with sorrow to the point of death. Stay here and keep watch with me.'" Matthew 26:37–38

Would you believe it! I just got off the phone with a senior programming executive at one of the television networks, and have I got a deal for you! They have agreed to let you confess your deepest, darkest secret on national television!

Pretty exciting, huh?

Yep, they are going to give you fifteen minutes, the amount of time Andy Warhol said each of us would be famous, to dance out the skeletons in your closet and rattle the bones to an audience of thirty million people.

What's that? You're not sure you want to take advantage of such an opportunity? You're not sure you're ready for that much exposure?

Wait a minute! Do you realize how tough it is to get through to these high-powered television types? I've gone to a lot of trouble to set this up. I don't think you appreciate how difficult this kind of negotiation can be.

But, that's okay. No, really. I did foresee just this sort of complication. I figured you might not like to reveal so much about your dark side. I understand. There are things I don't tell just anybody too. So I was able to persuade the programming people to agree to a fallback position.

Instead of sharing your greatest secrets, you can go on television and describe your deepest hurt. Tell them of that crushing need you've been reluctant to share with…anyone. You know, how difficult it is for you to feel good about yourself, how deep inside you don't really believe you're worth other people's caring about you. Or tell them how you have always longed for someone to love you. Your mom and dad were the reserved type—cool, unemotional, distant. So you have always needed nurturing, but you have never been able to tell anyone. Or talk about how lonely you feel sometimes, even when you're surrounded by people, even people you love. Tell them how you sometimes feel as if you are enveloped by cell walls three feet thick that nothing can penetrate—no human touch, no human emotion, nothing. Sure it might be painful to open up, but you know what they say: no pain, no gain.

You're not buying this, are you? You're about to chicken out on me. Well! Go ahead. But see if I go to this much trouble again. Some people can be so selfish and inconsiderate!

Or maybe you're just being human. Few of us are willing to open up and be vulnerable with complete strangers. In fact, the deeper the hurt, the darker the secret, the more protective and closed we tend to become. Even with those closest to us.

But is that wise?

WHAT WOULD JESUS DO?

While Jesus had no dark secrets to share, he certainly had a heart that was hurting at times. And he could have chosen any venue, any group to share it with. Or he could have kept his grief and pain only between himself and his Father.

Jesus was man and he was God, both, at the same time. He knew what it was like to have Satan tempt him, although he never gave in to that temptation; he never sinned. And Jesus had needs, needs that were both human and divine. He needed the comfort and presence of his Father. But what you might not have considered is that since Jesus was fully human he also needed the comfort and presence of his human friends. Remember Gethsemane?

JESUS IN THE GARDEN

There are only twelve of them now. The darkness had swallowed the thirteenth as he left the borrowed hall. Their stomachs are full; the wine has warmed them. The hour is late, and they long for the comfort of their thin pallets. All save one.

And the one who is not drowsy is troubled.

He leads them from the rough, upper room with its plaster-covered walls twice as thick as a man's body through the city gates and into the open, unlovable night. A dog barks in the distance. Another sings to the moon. These are the only sounds beyond the twenty-four sandaled feet slapping first on the dusty streets, then along the primitive road leading to the garden.

At the edge of Gethsemane the leader holds his right hand high in a silent command to stop. "John, Peter, James, come with me. The rest of you wait here."

The eight who remain nestle into softer places amid the clumps of grass and weeds, rocks and dust. This has happened before. Jesus needs to pray. And he's rarely quick about it. They might as well settle down for a nap. He may not return until dawn.

The four men continue deeper into the secluded garden. Stopping, Jesus says to them, "I am so sad I can hardly stand it. It's as if my soul is engulfed by grief, and it's killing me. I must pray. Stay awake and watch with me." With that, he retires a bit farther and falls to his knees. In agony he pleads with his Father to take this terrible burden from him.

To me this scene opens a window into the humanity of Jesus. He tells Peter, James, and John, straight up, in strong terms, that he is sad, his heart is breaking, and he wants them to keep watch with him. Here is the Son of God admitting he has pains and needs we don't associate with divinity. I thought God didn't need anything. I thought Jesus was a supernatural man. Yet at this most crucial time in his life he asks his closest friends to keep him company. The language he uses is strong and powerful. It is straightforward. "My soul is overwhelmed with sorrow to the point of death. Stay here and keep watch with me." Jesus bares his soul and opens his heart to them. By asking them to stay awake with him he is asking for their ongoing presence, their vigilance. He is asking them as his friends to be accountable to him and to share the burden of this moment.

That they didn't is heartbreaking. How tragic to be abandoned by those he loved. But I am so glad Jesus didn't wear a mask in the garden. Watching him in his distress gives me freedom. If he could be overwhelmed by sadness, feeling so heavy he thought he might die and be tempted to despair, why should I be surprised when I feel that way after a great loss? I think his human nature was behaving the way God intended all humans to behave during times of dire stress—first seeking guidance and comfort from his heavenly Father, then asking his close, trusted friends to "keep watch" with him. His humanity didn't preclude his need for God, nor did his divinity take away the needs of the man.

What a difference it makes to have a Savior who was both human and divine. It's not a concept our binary, black-and-white thinking minds handle easily. We can understand all man. All God we have no trouble with. But all man and all God at the same time seems riddled with inconsistencies.

But, then, my own reality is riddled with inconsistencies. I have devoted myself to Jesus Christ and living my life as he would live his. I trust him for everything. At the same time I worry about whether my IRA will be sufficient to provide the standard of living I "need" when I retire in twenty years. I plan and plot to make sure there will be sufficient money to give my sons the same education their sisters got. When I am embroiled in buying a piece of real estate or helping my sons start a small business, it's hard to think about Jesus. It's hard to consider God's will when the attorney is telling me to add an escape clause in case the deal goes south.

Seeing Jesus in the garden grappling with inconsistencies encourages me. I'm glad he didn't behave like a one-dimensional caricature of a man. It grieves me to see his pain, but it strengthens me in my own struggles with spiritual forces and with other people when I see Jesus praying so hard that his perspiration makes puddles in the dust on that cool April night. Yet he didn't succumb to the temptation to forsake it all. Rather, he said, "Abba, Father, everything is possible for you. Take this cup from me. Yet not what I will, but what you will" (Mark 14:36).

JESUS WANTED HIS FRIENDS CLOSE BY

At his greatest hour of need Jesus chose to have three of his closest friends nearby. I suspect there were several reasons. We know Jesus was concerned about their own susceptibility to sin and wanted to teach them about the dangers of temptations that were coming their way. Yet on a human level, I believe Jesus wanted to draw something from them, as well as impart something to them.

Jesus needed to talk long and hard with his Father about the bitter task ahead. Yet he didn't want to do it all alone. Other times he had retired to pray alone on a solitary peak, but this time he knew his hours of freedom were short.

Nor did he want to be surrounded by large crowds. I suppose he could have done the first-century equivalent of appearing on national television. He could have gone to the temple and gathered a crowd. "Hey, all you Jews—Pharisees, Sadducees, scribes, lawyers. Gather 'round. I have some tough praying to do and I want you to hear it."

Or he could have sailed up the coast to Antioch, the third most important city in the Roman Empire, and strolled into the circus between games to pray his prayer of anguish, hands held high, his head covered with his cloak.

Of course neither venue would have given him much human comfort. The director of the arena generally cared less about the participants than he did about the pacing of the show, much like some of today's television talk show hosts. And the Son of Man would have found the chief priests' levels of available compassion woefully short.

At the very least I suppose he could have allowed all the disciples to witness his prayer. But that, too, might have been catastrophic. Would they have wanted to fight for him? Would they have started a commotion, urging him to leave the area? Would they have fallen into despair as they beheld the grief flooding over their master? Would they have rushed to prove their loyalty, thereby disrupting his communion with God? Perhaps they would have tried to hustle him off under cover of darkness to some secret location. Any of these options would have been counter to Jesus' goals.

Jesus was in the middle of a deep grief, the kind best experienced with those we trust the most. When deep griefs are to be experienced, there is no room for masks. There is only room for close friends and God and his angels. So Jesus chose Peter and the two Sons of Thunder, James and John, to sit up with him.

This isn't the first time Jesus has called these three fishermen for special duty. He invited only the three of them to join him at the home of Jairus, the synagogue ruler, when he raised the man's daughter from death. He took them onto the Syrian mountain near Caesarea Philippi where they witnessed his transfiguration and heard the voice of God stamp his imprimatur on Jesus. And now he has asked them, apart from the others, to join him in the darkness of Gethsemane that mirrors the darkness of his soul.

Jesus is troubled. He is overwhelmed with sadness. He knows that in a very short time he will suffer betrayal, torture, degradation, and death at the hands of those he came to save. But more than that, he, who since before the beginning of time has always been in the Father's presence, will soon become that which the Father hates. Jesus will wrap himself in the sins of Moses and Abraham, Peter, James, and John, you and me and be separated from God for three days that will always mark the tapestry of eternity. The prospect of being cut off from the source of life for even so brief a time fills the Son of God with anguish impossible for us to comprehend.

Is it any wonder that Jesus wanted his closest friends by him then? The real wonder is they didn't understand better what was going on. That Peter, James, and John were not able to stay the course must have added to Jesus' sense of isolation and grief in the garden.

GOD CHAMPIONS RELATIONSHIP;
SATAN DELIGHTS IN ISOLATION

God is the author of relationships. It was God Almighty who created man and woman and placed them in the garden where he would walk to and fro in the cool of the evening, chatting with them. It was God who said, "It is not good for the man to be alone" and so created an appropriate partner for him.

The God who said, "Let us make man in our image, in our likeness" is a God of companionship (Genesis 1:26). There is inherent companionship in the Father, the Son and the Holy Spirit. And God desires a companionship with all of his creation. He enjoyed it with the first Adam during those halcyon days in Eden. After the Fall he chose companionship with sin-stained humanity through Jesus, the second Adam. In an act of divine paradox he decided he would rather face isolation from himself than isolation from his creation.

The Accuser, on the other hand, is the author of isolation. He destroys relationships. He is the one who tried to come between Jesus and his Father in the wilderness. And he is the one who tempted Peter, James, and John to forsake their Master and fall asleep in the garden, enhancing Jesus' sense of aloneness. And I believe he is responsible for tempting Jesus to the edge of despair in the garden. When the devil left Jesus in the wilderness, he went away waiting "until an opportune time" (Luke 4:13). What could have been more opportune than the eve of Jesus' arrest? And what victory he would have won had Jesus fallen prey to despair and hopelessness.

Our adversary wants us to feel isolated too. He likes for us to believe that no one can understand the pain we feel. And he loves it when we convince ourselves we are strong enough not to need the close fellowship of other people. Because the Father of Lies knows a lie when he plants one.

THE DANGERS OF SELF-SUFFICIENCY

He especially likes to encourage leaders to put themselves on pedestals. All Christians have been set apart for God's holy purposes, yet some leaders go to extremes. Convinced they have been chosen for special service to God, they believe they are not like other people. They do not need companionship or soul mates. Indeed, where can men and women without peer even hope to find a buddy? It is a powerful and seductive logic. It leads them to isolate themselves. They get to the point where they have only God in their inner circle. And some are even without him. So they become pushovers for temptations that parody intimacy. Like sexual sin.

I recently led a divorce recovery seminar at a church where three female participants had been married to pastors. Over the course of the seminar I learned that two of the men had been youth pastors who had affairs with members of their teenage flocks. The third was an older preacher who had engaged in multiple affairs with members of his various congregations.

All three men lacked intimate male friends. All of them lacked relationships that demanded accountability. And all of them felt as if their isolation was justified because of their holy position. No one could understand their special nature, and so they could get close to no one. Had they developed close relationships they likely would have seen what they did not believe was there: their own fallibility. But there was no need to be close to anyone else. They had convinced themselves of that.

And when they fell, each did his utmost to hide the sin. According to their wives and other observers, they blamed their spouses. They blamed their elders. They blamed their congregations for their lack of support. And they blamed the objects of their misdirected affections. They blamed God for not protecting them from such horrible evil. Publicly they blamed anyone but themselves. It seems their ultimate, unspoken goal was the impossible task of hiding their fall even from themselves.

It's a pattern of self-sufficiency that's far too common in the lives of believers. Hollywood has long stereotyped the self-righteous, self-sufficient patriarch with feet of clay. But this air of self-sufficiency is a lie. At their core these folks know they are not self-sufficient. They know their needs are immense. Yet if they allow others to come too close, their neediness might be noticed, and then their specialness will be in jeopardy. So they keep the mask of self-sufficiency in place. And like all masks, it separates them from the healing God intended the church to provide. And it allows Satan a sure way to trip them up.

At Oak Hills my fellow ministers and I recognized the dangers of sexual temptation in ministry several years ago. As we compared notes, we were all amazed to learn that this potent ministry breaker was not discussed in any of our academic training. Consequently we decided at least once a year to discuss at our weekly staff meeting the hazards of sexual temptations in each of our ministries. We discuss the costs of falling—how it would hurt our families, our church, and our own careers of God-ordained ministry. And we commit to one another to be available should anyone on staff need to talk about a temptation he is facing. We also covenant to confront each other if we see danger signals in one another's lives. That's a far different strategy from the one followed by the three ministers who fell.

Over the last twenty years I have seen others openly discuss the temptations of interoffice romance, hedging expense reports, cheating on income taxes, and more, all in the context of weekly small group Bible studies. These groups become environments where we can tell our stories to one another, confessing our sins, our temptations, and our victories. We become close to one another in these small groups. We choose to be vulnerable. And in the process we learn to love each other and become accountable to each other.

JESUS' CIRCLES OF INTIMACY

I think Jesus modeled much the same pattern. He had circles of intimacy—people to whom he revealed greater or lesser degrees of himself. The closer to the center, the greater the intimacy.

At the outer edge were the Gentiles, represented by the Syrophoenician woman, the demoniac of the Gerasenes, and the four thousand people Jesus fed near the Decapolis.

Then came the Jews, the group Jesus acknowledged he came

to save. There are many more instances of Jesus' revealing himself to the Jews, both his friends and his enemies, than to the Gentiles.

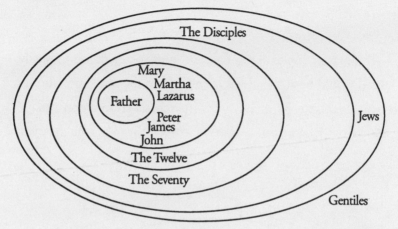

The disciples traveled with Jesus as camp followers, hanging on his words, basking in his radiance.

The seventy were sent out by Jesus to prepare the way for him, to heal the sick, and to have authority over the demons.

The twelve were his closest large group. He revealed to the apostles his reasons for using parables and gave them special understanding of the Kingdom.

But when he needed soul-sharing, intimate human contact, it most frequently came through two groups of people. Either it was with his friends from Bethany—Mary, Martha, and their brother, Lazarus. Or, more commonly it was with Peter, James, and John.

There is also strong evidence from the pen of John that Jesus had one special friend, the disciple whom he loved and to whom he entrusted the care of his mother after his death—John himself. We don't know the details of that friendship, but it seems to have gone beyond what Jesus had with the others.

OUR CIRCLES OF INTIMACY

We also have circles of intimacy. If I were to depict mine visually, God would be at the center because he is the one from whom I have no secrets. He is the one with whom I seldom don a mask. And even when I do, he can see through it. My wife, Mary, is

MY CIRCLES OF INTIMACY

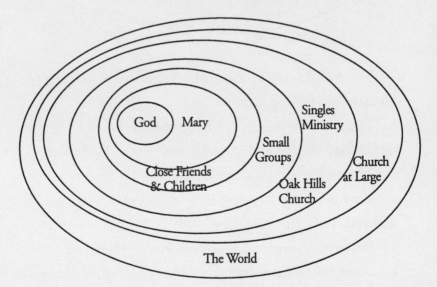

near the core. She sees more of the real me than anybody else on earth. Next come my children and my closest friends, of whom there are only two or three. After that are the two small groups I belong to: my fellow ministers and my Wednesday night Life

Group. They are followed by the single leaders, the singles ministry, the church at Oak Hills, the church at large, and then the "world."

Look at the strength in such a constellation of friends and acquaintances. By having varying levels of intimates, hiding from myself becomes a more arduous challenge. These people know me and will call me to account when I'm putting up a front. Conversely, when I have known the least about myself and when I have been closest to disaster have been the times I allowed my circles of intimacy to deteriorate.

An incident occurred several years ago which very few people know about. It was a time of great despair when I came close to committing suicide. I had consciously isolated myself from the church over a perceived slight. I kept my mask in place though, and no one was aware of either the slight or my spiteful, immature attempt at isolation. I had been depressed for some time. My business career was not providing the emotional strokes I needed. I had no close friends, except my wife. And I was traveling frequently.

On one trip, my last, I became so overwhelmed with a nameless despair that I seriously considered jumping out of the hotel window. I was both frustrated and thankful the hotel had only two stories. The first floor was half underground, and the property was out in the country, surrounded by nice soft grass and a thick blanket of pine needles and snow. If I had jumped, at the worst I could have broken a leg or sprained my ankle. That would have been more embarrassing than killing myself. When

I returned from the business trip, I sought professional help for my depression and found someone safe I could talk to about the things that were troubling me. Like most people who contemplate suicide, I didn't really want to die. I wanted an end to the pain.

But what really amazes me, in retrospect, is that I didn't have an affair. My profile at the time—a self-imposed isolation and wearing multiple masks—was perfect for an illicit liaison. But God was kind and constantly reminded me of how important my family was to me.

WHAT JESUS NEEDED IS WHAT WE NEED

How differently from me Jesus dealt with his emotional distress. And make no mistake, despite his divinity Jesus was in great distress. He was inundated by sadness. He felt like dying he was so sad. He needed to pray, to have intimate contact with God. But I believe the human side of Jesus wanted companionship too. He needed his friends to stand beside him as he prayed. As the anguish flooded over him, as his soul wept through the pores of his skin, he needed Peter, James, and John to be there for him, to support him with their presence. That they failed him in his time of need is a testimony to their fallibility, not to Jesus'.

Jesus had plenty of people around him while the Roman soldiers were beating and taunting him. There were crowds while he carried his cross. Even the disciples were in the audience on Skull Ridge when he was crucified. Yet the human comfort he desired in the garden could only come from the willing closeness of those with whom he had developed an intimate relationship. He couldn't get that from a temple full of Jews, a stadium full of arena watchers, or a national television audience.

What Jesus modeled in the garden is what you and I need: communion with God and the watchful presence of loving friends. God may not remove us from the pain. People may not be able to fix what's ailing us. But they can be there to share the moment, to hold our hand in the darkness, and to help us make it through the dark night of our soul.

LIFTING THE MASK

1. How would you feel about sharing your greatest needs with a national television audience?

2. When you feel needy, do you find someone to talk to about it, or do you handle it yourself? Why? To what extent does it depend on the depth of your need?

3. Do you agree that isolation puts a person at risk of succumbing to temptation? In what ways?

4. How do you feel about the idea that Jesus needed his friends in the garden? How does that affect your view of the Savior?

5. Read Matthew 26:38 again. Have you ever felt a "sorrow unto death"? Did you tell anyone? What happened?

6. What do you think leads to wearing a mask of self-sufficiency? Do you think it is a conscious process or one that is largely unconscious?

7. Sketch your circles of intimacy. What do you learn by seeing them on paper? Do you have the intimate resources you need to weather serious emotional storms?

Chapter 3

Face to Face with God

"And pray in the Spirit on all occasions with all kinds of prayers and requests." Ephesians 6:18

"Even now my witness is in heaven; my advocate is on high. My intercessor is my friend as my eyes pour out tears to God; on behalf of a man he pleads with God as a man pleads for his friend." Job 16:19–21

N o one models perfect communion with God the way Jesus does. We need that communion too. But unlike Jesus we have a problem. We're sinful, and our sin inhibits communion with our Father. Sin causes us to be dishonest. But deep relationships, both with God and with other human beings, require transparency, honesty. Sometimes that's painful or scary.

Even so, it's the very thing we were made for. Before God created a partner for the man, he created the man to relate to him in a unique way. He made human beings in his image, the only ones of his creation so made.

While Adam and Eve were still in the garden, it was God's

practice to stroll there in the cool of the evening and be with them. They walked. They talked. They had face-time with one another. The agenda: relationship.

When they surrendered to the temptation to do what God had commanded them not to do, they shattered the relationship and left it in the dust alongside their broken innocence. Then, out of fear and shame, they tried to hide.

Have you ever considered anything so ludicrous? Can you imagine them covering their naked bodies with hastily constructed aprons of fig leaves and hoping to mask themselves from the all-seeing, all-knowing Yahweh?

"Eve, look at you!" says the man.

"What?" she says, looking down, hands in the air.

"You're naked!"

Her hands drop instinctively, for the first time, to cover herself. "Well...yeah, but...hey, what about you? You're naked too, fella!"

"We're both naked. And God will notice! We've got to do something!"

"But what?" she asks as she edges behind a lush fig bush.

"Great idea, Eve!"

"Huh?"

"Those big green leaves...what did I call them?"

"Figs."

"Yeah, that's it. They're perfect. Let's make some clothes to cover up our naked parts."

"Do you think it'll work?"

"Sure. Just act like nothing's happened. He won't suspect a thing."

As if.

Would you notice if your son all of a sudden started wearing a full-head Halloween mask in July? Would you notice if your corporate executive mother began dressing in overalls, pretending to be a farmer? Would it be obvious to you if your best friend put a mole on her cheek, bleached her hair platinum, and began acting like Madonna? Would you notice?

Of course you would! The more familiar you are with someone the more aware you are of such charades.

God created us for open, honest contact with him, with no barriers, the way it was between him and the man and woman before the Fall. He knows everything there is to know about us. He knit us together when we were still in the womb. He understands us from the inside out. He realizes when we are covering up and pretending to be what we are not.

But that doesn't stop us, does it? We're about as subtle as Adam and Eve when we try to hide what we have done from the creator of the universe. And we're just as effective.

PRAYER CAN BE "HANGING OUT" WITH GOD

Mother Teresa is known for her praying. When she was interviewed by Dan Rather some time ago, he asked her, "What do you say to God when you pray?"

"I don't talk. I listen," she answered.

Rather smiled that bemused newsman's smile and asked,

"Well…what does he say to you?"

"Nothing. He mostly just listens."

Rather looked puzzled, and she continued, "And if you don't understand that, I can't explain it to you."

Perhaps I am being presumptuous, but I think I know what she meant. I think she "hangs out" with God.

I realize that sounds undivine, but hear me out. I call it "hanging out" because those words communicate the casual, nonagenda way we have of being in the presence of someone we love that, in a good way, takes the relationship for granted. A more theological way to say the same thing might be "to practice the presence of God."

When our two sons got old enough to appreciate their own personal space, we rearranged our house to provide each of them with a large bedroom, complete with a desk. We wanted them to have their own study space as they entered their teenage years. But they don't use their desks very much, except to collect clutter. When they study, they like to come to whatever room Mary and I are in because they still like just being with us.

The same holds true for me too. I love my boys and I truly enjoy their presence. Sometimes when they are watching cartoons on Saturday morning I'll go into the TV room to read or study, just so I can be with them. We don't talk. We're doing totally different things. It's almost like relationship by osmosis.

One of the lies we have told ourselves as a culture is that children need quality time more than quantity time. We believe that because it allows us to rationalize our workaholic ways and our decisions to do what we want—like spend our free time watching sports on TV or reading mystery novel after mystery novel—without truly considering the impact on our children. The fact is, quality time is an outgrowth of quantity time. Especially with kids. If you don't believe me, tell your child that you want to have fifteen minutes of "quality time" with him or her and see how high the quality really is. The quality moments are almost always pure serendipity, when our masks drop and circumstances allow pure honesty. In my family I find those quality moments happen most often when we are in the car running routine errands. Or when I'm helping with homework.

Mary and I can plan quality time with each other more than I can with the boys, but, even so, hanging out with her is what often feels the best. We are content just to be in the same room with each other. I'm reading a book and she's doing her needlepoint. Or she's reading and I'm paying bills. It is comforting to be in her presence.

How much more comforting to "hang out" with God, to rest in his presence.

I think that was what Mother Teresa was describing to Dan Rather. Her relationship with God is such that they can hang out together. They don't have to talk. She doesn't have to come with a great list of supplications. They are simply content in each other's presence. Together.

When we sin, our sin makes us unfit to be with God. Even though Jesus has died for our sins and his blood continually cleanses us, we act as if it hasn't. Our sin causes us guilt and shame because we know we have missed the mark and disappointed our Father.

But instead of confessing it to him, we do the ludicrous thing. We behave like Adam and Eve. We pretend it never happened, hoping God won't notice.

SIN CAUSES US TO HIDE FROM GOD

Like David in Psalm 32, we keep silent about our sin even though our bones waste away and we groan all day long. We get as far away from God as we possibly can. But the Hound of Heaven is persistent. He pursued the man in the garden. And his hand was heavy on David, as it is on us, sapping his strength until he acknowledged his sin to God. When David quit covering the perversity of his adultery with Bathsheba and the murder of Uriah and his men, God forgave him. God forgives us, too, when we confess our sins to him.

What Adam and Eve, and David, and I, and perhaps you, too, often forget is that God knows everything. Ev-er-y-thing. All of it. He knows what we are thinking about even before we do it. He knows when we don a mask, whether it comes up consciously or unconsciously. He knows that we are hiding, and he knows what we are hiding. And he pursues us until we come clean.

That's because God values the unique closeness of our relationship. After all, we are so important to him that he died rather than live without us. That's what the cross is all about.

It brings us close to him, closer than we could ever be on our own.

The sin we feel so guilty about would rightly separate us from the Holy God, for sin is the one thing he cannot tolerate. Yet, Jesus, the Paschal Lamb, took all of our sin to the cross, just as the ancient scapegoats carried the sins of Israel into the wilderness. And Jesus' sacrifice is a once-and-for-all sacrifice—the kind that keeps on cleansing even as we keep on sinning. It is as if when we rose from the watery grave of baptism that you and I got special Teflon coatings. The sins don't stick. So when we go to God in the quiet of our closets, in the stillness of our souls, Jesus is there to meet us. He wraps his arms around us. He absorbs the darkness of our hearts, the evil of our souls. And in its place he leaves his own light—clean, bright, and pure.

I don't understand it. I don't know how it really works. God's ongoing forgiveness is one of the many mysteries I can't unravel. But I do believe it happens. That is why we can do the truly horrible things we do and still be allowed to draw close to him.

WHERE SIN INCREASES, GRACE INCREASES ALL THE MORE

Speaking at a recent men's breakfast, Tony Campolo said, "The more unworthy you are, the more God loves you." While I might not put it that way, I would, however, say, "The more unworthy you are, the more God's love *works* for you." I believe that's what Paul was talking about in Romans: "where sin increased, grace increased all the more" (5:20).

Here's a test question: When does more of a parent's love come into play—when he or she is washing the dishes beside a sleeping infant or when the parent is cleaning him up after one of those terrible blowouts that disintegrates even the plastic lining of a disposable diaper? That's easy. One is intellectual love. The other is active. Boy, is it active.

Try this alternate question from the story of the lost son in Luke 15. Who is more in need of grace—the older brother who stayed home or the prodigal who rejected his father, turned his back on his home, lived a life designed to cause shame and embarrassment to all his living relatives, and then returned penniless and brokenhearted?

That's too easy.

Here's one more. Who do you suppose felt closer to his father? Was it the older son, who always had access to everything on his father's ranch, or the younger son, who had known poverty of pocket and spirit but who received incredible clothes and a great party when what he was expecting was a scathing tongue-lashing?

That's pretty much a no-brainer too.

Jesus gave Peter the same test, different question.

"'Two men owed money to a certain moneylender. One owed him five hundred denarii, and the other fifty. Neither of them had the money to pay him back, so he canceled the debts of both. Now which of them will love him more?'

"Simon replied, 'I suppose the one who had the bigger debt canceled.'

"'You have judged correctly,' Jesus said" (Luke 7:41–43).

Isn't that interesting. The one for whom grace was most

operative—the one with the greater debt—is the one who loves him more.

In the case of the two sons the older brother constantly received the grace and charity of his father. But extra grace was required for the younger son because he had strayed so far from an intimate relationship with his father. He had sinned mightily, and his sin drove him back into the arms of his father, full of contrition, full of confession.

The younger boy was amazed at his father's love and forgiveness. But it could only have been displayed after the young man's repentance and confession. And that came only with his pain. Until there was pain, there was no reason to drop his mask. His pain changed him. And so did his intimate moments with his father. Before he returned, he could only hope for a low paying job far from the big house. After his father received him, after the grace of the welcome home party, the errant child became the son once more.

PRAYER CHANGES US

Prayer is one of the ways we develop intimacy with God. Prayer changes us as surely as intimacy with another person changes us.

Intimacy gives us the freedom to show our weaknesses, our vulnerability. We have the freedom to drop our masks and learn who we are—creatures of God, intended for his righteous service and all the good he has planned for us. To keep our masks in place, to pretend we have no need for intimacy with God is the height of foolishness.

And it cuts us off from the source of all strength.

When Jesus came down from the mount of transfiguration, he found a frustrating situation. A boy's father was frustrated with Jesus' disciples, and Jesus' disciples were frustrated with an evil spirit who had been afflicting the young boy. It was a particularly evil demon who would seize control of the boy, rob him of his speech, throw him to the ground, and cause him to become rigid, gnash his teeth, and foam at the mouth. It was a terrible torment that deprived him and his family of joy and any semblance of a normal life (Mark 9:14–29).

The father had brought his son to Jesus' disciples, hoping they might heal him. But their efforts were fruitless.

When Jesus came on the scene, he shook his head at their ineptitude, then quickly sent the demon away shrieking.

When they got together away from the crowd, he explained to his followers that this kind of demon, this degree of demonization, could be dealt with effectively only through prayer.

Yet Jesus did not pray before he sent the demon packing.

Why not?

Jesus was never under any delusions about the source of his power. He always relied on the power of the Holy Spirit when he healed the sick or cleansed people of evil spirits. Even at the Last Supper he held both the bread and the wine up to God, blessing him for his provision.

The disciples were not so well focused. As normal human beings, like you and me, they looked in mirrors and walked away not remembering what they looked like. It might not have been a difficult twist of their rational apparatus to conclude that they themselves had a lot to do with the miracles God performed through them when Jesus sent them out in pairs. It would have been easy to believe it was their faith, their integrity, their forcefulness of character that allowed God to work in them.

These guys needed to pray because prayer provides close, personal contact with the Father, and by praying they remembered who they were, and who he is. Without prayer it is likely they could have fallen back on their own capabilities. With prayer they were breaking down any possible barriers that would keep the power of God from working through them.

Isn't that what prayer does in our lives, too?

I go to God, sometimes full of myself, sometimes frustrated at the behavior of others, and he changes me. He fills me with himself. He refocuses me to him and his desires for my life.

Mystical? You bet!

Magical? Not a chance!

The process is mystical. How it works, I don't know. But it's not magical. Magical is when I confuse God with the genie in the lamp. Magical is when I try to manipulate the supernatural for my own purposes.

Mystical is why God, in his supreme authority, would take time even to hear what I have to say, let alone act upon it. Mystical is why that same God, instead of changing things around me will change me at my heart level. Mystical is why Yahweh would even countenance intimacy with me, let alone desire it.

Heaven is the ultimate intimacy with the Father. There we

will sit beside the throne, at his feet, always in his presence. There will be no masks, only honesty. There will be no darkness, only light. No pain, only joy. Prayer gives us a taste of that intimacy with our Father. In a very real sense, prayer is heaven on earth.

LIFTING THE MASK

1. What do you think it means for two people to be intimate? How is intimacy achieved? What does it take to destroy intimacy?

2. Have you ever tried to hide something from someone you cared for deeply? What was that like for you? How did it affect your relationship?

3. Have you ever had someone you cared for try to hide from you? What was that like? What was the impact on your relationship?

4. What do you think of the concept of "hanging out" with God? How would you explain Mother Teresa's comment?

5. David said that when he kept silent before God about his sins his bones wasted away, he groaned all day long, his strength was sapped. Have you found that to be true in your experience or in observing the experiences of others? What happens when we finally confess our sin to God?

6. How does praying help us to become intimate with God?

Chapter 4

Where Do Masks Come From?

"He reveals deep and hidden things; he knows what lies in
darkness, and light dwells with him."
Daniel 2:22

Rhonda[1] was weeping in my office. Her middle-aged face
was swollen and red and pieces of cheap tissue, disinte-
grated by her tears, were sticking to her cheeks.

Looking past me at some point beyond the wall, she had just
told me about the man who had raped her when she was in her
early twenties. She had gone to him for his professional exper-
tise, and he had taken advantage of her youth and her vulnerability. He had wormed his way into her confidence and gained
control over her in a most despicable way.

For over twenty years she had masked the incident from her
conscious mind. She had buried it deep with all the grief and
shame that went with it. And now, in the process of talking
about her depression and her feelings of alienation from God,
the terrifying images had bubbled to the surface, bursting their
deferred pain over her.

As we continued talking, she said with a note of hushed awe in her voice, "I'm telling you things I didn't even know I knew!"

"Telling me things she didn't even know she knew." How does such a thing happen? How can we mask off a part of ourselves and not even know we are doing it? How can pain be partitioned off in this way? What are the conscious and unconscious masks we wear?

KNOWN BY YOU, KNOWN BY OTHERS

Imagine a four-paned window on the wall of your front room. Now imagine your name in big bold type above it. This window

YOUR NAME

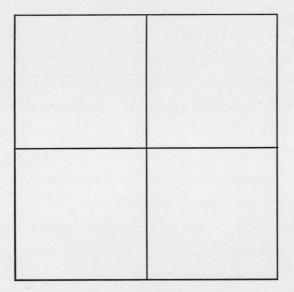

represents everything there is to know about you. It holds simple facts about you as well as how you operate, what you feel, what you fear, what you love, and what you hate. In it are all your memories and all that has happened to you. This model of self-disclosure is called the Johari Window, named after its two creators, Drs. Joseph Luft and Harry Ingham.

In the upper left quadrant is what you know about yourself and what others know about you. This includes physical characteristics that are fairly obvious, such as your hair color, if you walk with a limp, or if you have bags under your eyes. It also includes your favorite color and whether you like to go to parties and meet new people.

KNOWN BY YOU, NOT KNOWN BY OTHERS

In the lower left quadrant is information you know about yourself but others don't know. This includes, but is not restricted to, events that happened outside of someone else's experience, such as childhood memories you have not shared, or vacations you took by yourself, or the nights you spent studying alone in the library. It also includes secrets you want no one else to know, including secret sins.

Our conscious masks operate out of these two panes. When we choose to hide what we feel, what we think, or what we believe ourselves to be, we are masking off part of these windows.

NOT KNOWN BY YOU, KNOWN BY OTHERS

Often others know things about you of which you are not yet aware. For instance, I might know that you respond defensively to criticism—something you not only don't know but would respond defensively to if I were so brash as to bring it to your attention. Or I might know that you are getting gray hair or gaining weight when these happy bits of knowledge have not yet dawned on you. I might be aware that you are burdened by pride, while that very pride requires that you remain blissfully ignorant of the fact. However, I may also see your ability to relate to children, your love for the unlovable, and your willingness to go the extra mile in difficult situations—characteristics which you may not recognize in yourself. This is all represented by the upper right pane of the window.

The more intimate we become with one another, the larger the upper two panes can grow because intimacy is about knowing people. Yet, the masks we wear keep us from knowing ourselves and from being known by others. By their nature, masks inhibit intimacy.

THE JOHARI WINDOW

Known by me Known by others	Not known by me Known by others
Known by me Not known by others	Not known by me Not known by others

NOT KNOWN BY YOU,
NOT KNOWN BY OTHERS

The final pane, the lower right, holds the secret information that no human being, including yourself, knows about you. This is where Rhonda had stored the memories of her rape.

All this is the province of God. He is the one who knows all our secrets. "Nothing in all creation is hidden from God's sight. Everything is uncovered and laid bare before the eyes of him to whom we must give account" (Hebrews 4:13). He knows everything in all the panes, but he exclusively knows the fourth pane.

That's no surprise to us. Of course God knows everything about us. He has experienced our lives with us with his eyes attuned to all levels—physical, emotional, and spiritual. As we are coparticipants with Christ, Christ is a coparticipant with us. Everything we know, he knows. But he knows more. He knows those secret things about us which even we don't know. He knew about Rhonda's assault even when she no longer remembered it. And I believe God was responsible for her learning about it after all those dormant years.

It makes sense that if our loving Father thinks we need to become aware of something in this pane, he will send his Holy Spirit to guide us and counsel us. Or he may place us in a relationship with another person that demands vulnerability. He may also allow us to experience trials in order to reveal our hidden strengths or weaknesses.

The panes in our windows are not rigidly set. Rather, they vary in size and shape depending on whom we are with. When

I am with my wife, my upper left window is quite large and the lower left window is small. Even after seventeen years of marriage, there are still things I know about me that Mary doesn't, but no other human being knows me as thoroughly as she does. If my audience changes to you, however, my upper left pane becomes much, much smaller, even though you may have the impression of knowing me well from reading my work.

MY WINDOW WITH MARY

Known by me Known by Mary	Known only by Mary
Known by me but not Mary	Not known by me Not known by Mary

THREE REASONS FOR LIMITING INTIMACY

Three factors influence how large the two left panes will be relative to an audience. One is our comfort with the audience. How safe do I feel with you? How much power do you have to cause me harm or to do me good? And how likely are you to use what

I reveal to harm me or to help me? There is always risk in self-disclosure, but without it, relationships cannot develop.

The issues of comfort and safety cannot always be answered on a purely conscious level. Rhonda, for instance, had long felt uneasy in the presence of men who were in the same profession as her attacker. She never understood why, however, until she began to cry in my office.

But in most circumstances we can be deliberate and calculating about what we reveal to others. We weigh the risk of uncovering against the rewards of getting close to another human being, much as an investor weighs the risks of an investment against the potential rewards. If we perceive the rewards to outweigh the risks, we reveal more of ourselves. If in our minds the risks outweigh the rewards, either we say nothing or we attempt to circumvent the risks by putting on a mask and only pretending to show ourselves.

A good example of how we work through these processes can be seen in how I decide what personal revelations to include in my writing. Take the story of my request for prayers for my disintegrating marriage in 1973. In certain fellowships such a revelation by a minister would mean an end to his active ministry, even if, as in my case, the incident occurred over a dozen years prior to the beginning of the ministry. That would mean a loss of career and livelihood. It might preclude career advancement or working with another congregation. Yet, because I have no aspirations to move to a different church, and because little of my income derives from my work in ministry, little could be done to hurt me in this regard. True, my congregation could reject me, but even that is doubtful since I am ministering in the congregation where the incident took place. Many of the people who were in the assembly that December Sunday are still members of this church. There is no new information here for them, only reminders of a body of believers who rallied to the pain and despair of one of its young members. So I didn't have to risk much in sharing this story with you.

Another factor is our own comfort with what we are revealing about ourselves. Have we been able to accept it ourselves? If so, we are much more likely to be willing to reveal it to others. It seems Rhonda had found the violation of her rape so repugnant that she had never become comfortable enough with it even to acknowledge it had happened. As a result, she couldn't share it with anyone else.

The third factor that influences how large the two left panes will be is the amount of time we spend with one another. Mary knows so much about me because I spend more time with her than with anyone else. Relationship is time sensitive. If we don't spend time together, we won't have the opportunity of knowing each other very well. Absence may make the heart grow fonder, but out of sight is often out of mind.

When we spend time with another person, we reveal ourselves both consciously and unconsciously. We present information with our words, of course, but our bodies and the way we speak tell even more. Sometimes others even learn things about us that we don't know—prejudices we hold, blind spots we have.

I once met an inventor, a scientist who had meticulously documented every major business encounter he had ever had. He concluded that if he spent an intensive six to eight hours with someone, he would know enough to decide whether he wanted to do business with that person or not. He would have learned about the person's integrity, honesty, and what was important to him or her. As a result, when he was considering any major business relationship, he engineered it so he could have at least six uninterrupted hours with the people involved.

As a relationship grows, we get to know more, not just about each other but about ourselves as well. We dis-cover that which was there all along but which was hidden from our sight. This "aha!" response in learning about ourselves reduces the size of the two right panes of the window and enlarges the two left panes. At times we all have experienced that sense of discovery in our close relationships—a true sense of learning something new and profound. I believe God uses relationships to reveal those hidden things about ourselves that he wants us to know.

That's what happened with Rhonda through our counseling relationship. When we first met, she was closed up and shut down, emotionally. Her lower left window pane was tiny. Her standard face presented a big, toothy smile, even when she was in great pain. The smile was her ever-present mask.

Over a period of several weeks we got to know each other. She learned she could trust me. She began to smile less and cry more. And only when she felt safe was she free to lower the mask she didn't even know she was wearing.

For over twenty-five years Rhonda had kept the darkness inside where it festered and fermented, silently poisoning her relationships with men. It is significant that God allowed her to recall the unpleasant event only in the safety of a relationship with another believer. Only when she felt she would not be hurt did God allow her to drop her mask and begin dealing with the pain of the ancient assault.

Rhonda's window of self-disclosure was opened in the context of a counseling relationship. Yet God does the very same thing through our relationships with other Christians.

As we get to know them and learn their trustworthiness, we find the freedom to lower our guard, peel the mask up, and risk letting them see the real us. They in turn do the same, and then the *koinonia*, the intimate fellowship God intended for the church, begins to blossom.

LIFTING THE MASK

1. On a piece of paper sketch your own window. How large is your upper left pane compared to the bottom left pane? What does this say about your willingness to let others know you?

2. Has anyone ever told you something about yourself that you were not aware of? How did you feel? How did it help you to learn about yourself?

3. What has God shown you that was buried in the lower right pane of your Johari Window?

4. How did he arrange for you to discover it?

5. If you wanted to open up your lower left pane, how could you do it? With whom would you begin?

Chapter 5

When It Hurts Too Much to Pray

"I urge, then, first of all, that requests, prayers, intercession and thanksgiving be made for everyone—for kings and all those in authority, that we may live peaceful and quiet lives in all godliness and holiness." 1 Timothy 2:1–2

I hate certified letters.

You know it's bad news the minute you get one. And worse still, you know that someone is trying to cover his backside. That's what that "return receipt requested" means. "See! We delivered it. He got it. We did our part and we can prove it. He can't weasel out of it now!"

So when I had lugged in the last bag after arriving home from our ski vacation and noticed the yellow "We Attempted Delivery" slip amidst all the "You have won...!" envelopes and the late Christmas cards, my stomach automatically dropped to my knees and hung there like a rock. The yellow slip said it was from the Department of Counseling. Since the post office isn't open on Sunday afternoons, I had to wait until half past eight the next morning to learn what was so earth-shattering that the school faculty had to send it in this special, ominous way.

Only a few years ago I had retired from business to go into singles ministry full time. My wife and I both believed that was where God was leading me, so after much prayer and reflection, we took the plunge. I quickly realized that ministry brings you in close proximity to people, many of whom have problems—emotional problems, financial problems, sexual problems, relationship problems, problems with the families they grew up in, problems with the church. The list is like a black hole: there is no end.

My education had not prepared me to minister to such a broad range of personal predicaments. I had received my undergraduate degree in broadcasting, not ministry and not counseling. I felt inadequate, to say the least. But God had also given me gifts of mercy and compassion and a burden to help people. And he had given me experiences that tempered me for this difficult work. So again after much prayer and some fasting, I decided to go back to school and get an advanced degree in counseling. The school I chose had a reputation for teaching and developing the skills I felt I needed.

For three and a half years I had been pursuing this course, squeezing classes into an impossible schedule, just like most other more "mature"—translate that "older"—graduate students. I had done well, maintaining an A average, which is not a unique accomplishment for "nontraditional" students like me. Older students tend to be more motivated, I think.

So why would they be writing me a certified letter? The department hadn't sent me more than two pieces of mail in the three years I had been there. At times I wondered if they even knew my address. And now a certified letter. I told myself not to worry until I picked up the letter the next day. But myself told me to forget it. I didn't sleep well that night.

And for good reason.

I couldn't believe the letter when I opened it at 8:45 Monday morning in the post office parking lot. "Based on deficiencies during CN 7380 Internship I, the MFT faculty is placing you on probation from Internship. Further enrollment in the Internship sequence will be denied until you remediate the deficiencies to the satisfaction of the faculty, as detailed below." The letter went downhill from there.

I was devastated. Never in my entire academic career had I received a grade lower than a C, and that was in high school physics, which is completely understandable. Calculus could just as easily have done me in if I had been crazy enough to take it.

But here they were, telling me I had failed my first semester of internship. Internship is where you actually begin seeing clients and using the skills you have learned. I had been weighed in the balance and found wanting.

I was angry. Enraged. How dare they!

And I was scared. What would the elders think? What would my fellow ministers think? What would my friends in the singles ministry think? What would the people I had been counseling say when they found out the school thought I was inadequate? What about the Christian clinic I had been working with? How would those psychiatrists, psychologists, and psychotherapists feel when they realized I wasn't as good as they and I thought I was.

Even if the school was mistaken, and I had good reason to believe they were, I could see the waves crashing across every area of my life. I would not be able to finish my program in my forty-fifth year as I had planned. I might not be able to finish at all!

The news was such a shock to my system that I reverted to primitive defenses. In the middle of writing a book on dropping our masks, I planted one firmly over my face. I clammed up, closed up, shut up. I told no one but Mary, and for the first time in our marriage I swore her to secrecy. She could tell no one, not even her mother or her sister.

That first couple of days I had meetings with the faculty, meetings which only magnified my sense of dread and loss. Nothing I said made any difference. None of their misunderstandings mattered. Nor did it matter that they had made their decisions in an information vacuum. It was like the law of the Medes and Persians: what the king had written not even the king could rescind—even if the king was wrong.

I came home and cried. Sometimes the tears were silent. Sometimes they were loud. Sometimes there was audio and no video. I didn't want anyone to see me. I didn't want anyone to touch me, not even Mary. And when she did, I wept without control. I retreated as far as I knew how. And for a time I just curled up in my chair and slept.

As I burrowed into the recliner, shutting Mary and the rest of the world out, she wouldn't cooperate. She kept intruding.

Okay, it wasn't exactly intruding. She sat close to me and put her hand on my shoulder. I couldn't take it. I felt so miserable and alone, so unloved and unlovable, that when she touched me the floodgates burst. My tears began to stream, and I had great difficulty catching my breath.

After the sobs subsided, she asked if she could pray for me. "Okay. But don't expect me to join in. I can't," I replied.

And so she did. There was a lightening of the load, and I felt better for a while.

Mary told me it seemed like a spiritual attack. I tended to agree, but it didn't really matter. When you've been hit by an eighteen-wheeler, it doesn't matter whether it has Mayflower or Spirit Movers written on the side. You're just as flat.

Eventually I climbed out of the chair, crawled into the car, and headed for the interstate. I drove. I drove with tunnel vision, seeing only enough to keep from having an accident. While white lines slapped by the car, I remembered a youth minister at a local congregation who had disappeared one day several years ago, and I thought about the credit cards in my wallet and the money in the bank and the proximity of the airport and the length of the interstate. But I knew I couldn't outrun the pain. I knew I couldn't outrun the shame. And I knew I could never tell another soul what I was feeling and fearing.

I tried to pray, but the prayers either came out as angry accusations, or they got stuck in my throat. I was lower than a snake's belly in Death Valley. And I was afraid to let anyone get close enough to lift me up.

I get queasy now, thinking what might have happened if my circles of intimacy had been as empty as they had been several years earlier. But they weren't. I needed those people now. I needed them to intercede for me. I needed them to accept me. I needed them to listen without judging. And later, when I could hear them, I would need them to tell me if they thought the action was warranted.

I knew I needed them, all right. But with the exception of Mary I couldn't let anyone in.

The next day I went back to work. But little work was done. My friends came by to say hi. I must have looked pretty bad because each asked how I was doing. I didn't lie. I just told them, "Not very well. But it's nothing I want to talk about right now."

Glen Carter, the counseling minister, wouldn't let it end there. As Mary had placed her hand on my shoulder, Glen placed his hand on my heart with his presence. And so I risked dropping the mask and letting him see what had happened. He didn't hate me. He didn't say, "Well, that tears it, Toombs. You'll never counsel in this church again." Instead he listened and then he prayed for me. He went to God for me when I couldn't go for myself.

Glen didn't gloss over what I was feeling and pretend everything was okay. It wasn't. He did say honest, supportive things like, "I don't agree with them, and I don't understand how they can take the position they have taken." But he didn't try to fix things. He was a good friend. He was there.

And then I succumbed to one of those slimy satanic tricks. I began to discount Glen's response. Of course he would say those things. He was a trained counselor. He was also one of my oldest friends. Like Mary, he had to accept me. And the fact was, it felt terrible to let the mask slip, even with him.

Later I had to meet with Michon, one of the church secretaries. We have a special friendship because of her status as a single mom and my work as the singles minister. We met in my office and conducted the business that absolutely could not wait.

Then Michon said I didn't look very good. Did I need to talk?

I turned away from her and lied, "No. But please go now." It had taken more energy than I realized to keep the mask up and the pain and grief at bay for our ten-minute visit. I couldn't do it any longer.

"Well, at least can I give you a hug?" she asked.

"Sure," I replied. My voice was wooden and so was my body. And then she, to whom I had given comfort on many occasions, hugged me. My tears began to flow. Sobs came coughing from deep within my chest. Bless her heart, she never asked for an explanation or gave a single word of advice. She just stood there silently praying for me until I was ready to stop, and then she quietly went back to her office.

ADMINISTERING GOD'S GRACE

Tom Vermilion, a singles minister and friend in Midland, says that Christians have two basic functions, the priestly and the prophetic. The prophetic is the one where we yank on someone's chain and help him or her get back on the right path. It's what many nonbelievers associate with Christians and church.

But it was the priestly function that Michon and Glen and Mary performed for me. And it is the one Jesus performed for the woman caught in adultery, and the woman who washed his feet with her tears at Simon the Pharisee's house, and the woman at the well who had been married to so many different men. Although he admonished two of these women, what stands out most starkly in each of these situations is how he administered grace to all of them.

That's what my friends did for me. They administered God's grace when I couldn't do it for myself. I couldn't pray for myself. I couldn't read the Bible. I could hardly love myself so deep was my sense of failure and rejection and loss. It seemed as if my entire spiritual and emotional systems had been short-circuited. I was unable to petition the throne on my own behalf.

This is not an unusual circumstance. It is one of the reasons God created the church. Both Paul and Peter teach about the importance of administering God's grace to one another.

Paul reminds the Ephesians that he was given the task of administering grace through preaching the good news to the Gentiles, which included them. If he hadn't preached to them, they might never have known the salvation that was being offered them. They might have remained lost in their sins, forever isolated from God. But because he showed them God's grace, the demons themselves were put on notice that the game had changed forever, that no longer were God's chosen people to be taken only from Israel (Ephesians 3:2–12). Now they would come from a "new Israel," those whose very hearts had been circumcised. This new group of people he christened the church, those called out from the normal ambitions and struggles of the world into a new way of living and walking. And this new church would work God's will by loving one another, by bearing one another's burdens, and by interceding in prayer for one another.

Likewise, Peter exhorts the brethren to use whatever gifts the Holy Spirit has given them to serve each other. It is through these acts of Christian service that God's grace is administered to his people. "If anyone speaks, he should do it as one speaking the very words of God. If anyone serves, he should do it with the strength God provides, so that in all things God may be praised through Jesus Christ" (1 Peter 4:10–11). God is praised when we intercede for one another. Glen and Michon and Mary were praising God when they were standing in the breach for me. And when you stand in the breach for your brothers and sisters, your very acts of Christian charity praise his name.

That's what interceding is. It is standing in the breach. My wall had been broken, and the enemy had been given entry. In my weakened state I was unable to stop his advances. But my friends could. And they did. And I began to appropriate a bit of his grace. I experienced his love as he intended it to be experienced—within the fellowship of those called by his Son's name. Each of them—my wife, my friend, my secretary—is a priest of God Most High. And each of them performed the priestly function Jesus intended by administering portions of his grace. And with each bit of grace administered I gained more comfort, and more courage, and more strength.

It was another week before I dared reveal the situation to the other ministers. Understand, please, that I knew they would not reject me. I know those fine men better than that. But I also feared...they might. I feared they might somehow decide I was no longer worthy to work alongside them. It is the most diabolical of Satan's schemes to make us believe we are not worthy of love and acceptance from those with whom we have developed loving and accepting relationships. So we feel we must withdraw from them before they withdraw from us. But what Satan intends for evil, God translates to good.

Each of the men was as compassionate with me as he would have been with any other member of the congregation. Perhaps even more so. One of them shared a similar thing that had happened to him, and he understood how devastating it could be. Each in turn ministered to me. They all gathered around and placed their hands on me, as is our custom, and then interceded with God on my behalf. I thank God that I allowed them to do it. The more I let my mask down, the more I risked myself with others, the stronger I became.

And the more willing I became to reveal the problem to my Life Group and the Singles Core Group, the people to whom I am closest in my ministry.

WHEN THE MASK FALLS, OTHERS BENEFIT TOO

It is interesting that I was not the only one who was strengthened by this ugly affair. God is much more efficient than that.

I first noticed a change in my fellow ministers. They seemed more willing to talk about personal struggles and problems during our meetings together. It seemed, too, that more praying took place between these men in the weeks that followed. While it is quite common to see two of them together with their heads bowed, praying for one another, these occasions appeared more frequent in the aftermath of my confession.

Then, too, there were changes in my Life Group. Pat, the minister in charge of our small groups, had lunch some time later with one of the men from our Wednesday night group. When Pat asked him how things were going, the man reported the Life Group had become much closer than it had ever been. "Why do you think that's true?" Pat asked. "Because Jim has been opening up more lately. He's been sharing more of his life with us, and that has given us courage to do the same."

In fact, they did the same thing. For weeks afterwards there was much more sharing, many more requests for prayer, and more praying for one another than there had been before. My vulnerability had freed others to lower their shields and be more vulnerable. Transparency throughout our small group increased.

THE CHURCH—GOD'S HEALING INSTRUMENT

It is a wondrous thing to behold the healing hand of God. His mercy overflows. And so does his efficiency. At the same time he heals one, he makes it possible for others to draw closer to him and to one another. When I peeled away my self-protection, I ended my self-imposed exile. I was blessed with intimacy and acceptance from the church. And the church was blessed by the opportunity to minister to me. They were also encouraged to share their own struggles, their own pain. I was surprised at the number of similar academic horror stories I heard from Christians of all ages. And most of them started with the preamble, "I've never told anybody else about this, but...."

As a young man I often questioned God's wisdom in creating the church. Why didn't he just whisk us off to heaven still wet from our rebirth? Why did he force us to be involved in the church? Why did he require that we have relationship with other imperfect but saved human beings? Sometimes they disappoint us and sometimes we disappoint them. On occasions they even treat us badly and hurt us. And, in turn, we hurt our brothers and sisters in the church, too.

God knew that sort of thing would happen when he called us out and pulled us all together. He knows how imperfect we are. And he knows how much we need each other. As much as we can, he wants us to love one another here the way we will love one another in Paradise, openly and without masks. Loving means trusting and encouraging. And it means going to the throne of our heavenly Father for one another, especially when the wounded Christian is too hurt to pray for himself.

With masks there can be no intercession. Without intercession, Satan gains a sure and certain victory. But with intercession, he is defeated and the name of God is praised. Christians are strengthened. They become emboldened. God is glorified. And the demons are reminded once again who is really in charge.

LIFTING THE MASK

1. How has bad news come for you? How have you reacted—with transparency or by donning a mask?

2. Did you ever find the courage to talk about your bad news with other Christians? How?

3. How does it benefit people to know when others are praying for them?

4. If we are priests who have access to God's throne, why would God tell us to pray for each other? Why would it not be sufficient merely to pray for ourselves?

5. If you have never dropped that mask of self-protection, is there someone with whom you can lower it now who would be willing to intercede in prayer for you? What would it take for you to risk trusting him or her enough to lower your mask?

Chapter 6

The Power of Confession

"If we confess our sins, he is faithful and just and will forgive us our sins and purify us from all unrighteousness." 1 John 1:9

"He who conceals his sins does not prosper, but whoever confesses and renounces them finds mercy." Proverbs 28:13

Acknowledging need is important, as Jesus demonstrated in the garden. But often buried with our needs in the lower left pane of our Johari Windows are the sins we have committed that we have never shared either with God or with another individual. Unmasking them, confessing them, becoming transparent about them can be difficult indeed.

If you're like me, the word "confession" conjures images of ornately carved, dark, wooden closets in ancient cathedrals. The penitent believer approaches the polished cubicle in the near darkness, fumbles with the latch, and pushes back the door. Inside is a cramped nook with a circular metal grating midway up the far wall. The grate glows with light from the other side as the believer kneels on the padded rail, her mouth at just the right level for speaking into the grate.

"Father, forgive me for I have sinned. It has been seven days since my last confession." Only the words travel to the other side, carried on the waves of the anonymous voice.

A dark-robed figure sits quietly in the gloom, listening and praying, and then responds. "Tell me, my daughter, what you wish to confess."

The confession continues from the shadows beyond the grate. "Father, I have been rude to my son. Sometimes he makes me so mad. And I have been angry with my husband for no reason. And I have been having lustful thoughts about a man at work...." So with painful words the believer begins to recount her sins since her last confession. When she is done, the nameless priest, with compassion and without judgment, pronounces the penance to be done. "My child, your penance is to say five Hail Marys, three Our Fathers, and ten rosaries. Now go and sin no more."

And so the act of confession goes, millions of times each week in the Catholic church. The unspeakable is confessed by the unknown to be heard by the unnamed.

VULNERABILITY IS THE KEY

My Catholic friends tell me that some of the younger priests often ask if the confessors would like to talk face to face with them, especially if the sins they are confessing are complex and particularly painful.

Why would they do that?

Perhaps they recognize that the anonymous confessional loses its power since it includes neither vulnerability nor accountability.

Vulnerability is essential to spiritual healing, and it runs counter to the basic human desire to self-protect. Without vulnerability both parties are "protected." The priest avoids having to personalize the confessed sins to a specific individual. And without an individual to relate them to, the priest's relationships with his parishioners can remain relatively untouched by the confessions he hears. The next time he sees Mr. Jones, who cheated on his income taxes, he may not make the connection. And if he does, the rules say he should pretend he doesn't in order to preserve Mr. Jones's anonymity.

As for the confessors, when they see the priest outside the confessional, they can pretend they really aren't sinners. They're OK and the priest is OK—so long as nobody says anything. So long as no one mentions the confessed sins, the charade of righteousness continues.

Vulnerability implies accountability. And both parties lose the benefits of accountability when confession is handled anonymously. For instance, if I risk being vulnerable with you and confess a lifelong problem with arrogance, part of the implied contract between us is you may ask me, "Jim, how are you doing? Has the Lord given you victory over what we prayed about?"

And of course that is precisely what I am afraid you will do. Because then I will have to confess again if I have fallen, or I will hide behind my mask of righteousness and lie, maintaining our relationship only on the surface while fracturing it at the deeper, more meaningful levels. "He sure has, Alice. Everything is right as rain. Speaking of rain, think we'll be getting any soon?"

HIDING SIN DESTROYS
BOTH THE SINNER AND THE CHURCH

How different from the early church. When they met, they shared all things in common. They ate meals together. They sang hymns and prayed together. And they confessed their sins to one another. Then they continued eating and singing and praying together.

Confessing sins had been a practice of God's community from the beginning of the Jewish law. Moses told the people in Leviticus 5:5 to confess their sins whenever they violated the laws God had given. Under the old law, this confession was to God, even when the leader was confessing for the people, as did Moses, Nehemiah, Ezra, and Daniel. Christians, though, are given the additional directive to confess to one another.

Paul's converts in Ephesus confessed their involvement with the occult and made a bonfire of their writings (Acts 19:18–19). James not only encourages believers to confess to one another but says that confessing to each other and praying for each other can result in healing (James 5:16). Why? Isn't it enough to confess to God? Why does James tell us to confess to one another?

Perhaps James understood the disease of denial and the tempting trap of hypocrisy more than others. After all, as the brother of Jesus he had been closer to Jesus than most of the other disciples and for much longer. Yet, along with his other brothers and sisters, he at first refused to acknowledge Jesus as the Son of Man. Then he ultimately made the journey of faith and became one of the pillars of the church in Jerusalem. I believe his exhortations to the Jews who had dispersed during the persecution were drawn from his own experiences at hiding the obvious. James knew how transparent the church had been following Pentecost, and now he was reminding them that even though they were in strange lands with strange, Gentile believers, they were still called to the same standards of community. These new believers were not the people they had grown up with down the street. They weren't their blood relatives. But James reminds them they are just as much their brothers and sisters in Christ as were the Jewish Christians they left behind.

I also believe James had a deeper understanding of the reality of the church as the body of Christ. When we confess to one another, we are confessing to God. After all, we are the body of Christ, and where two or three are gathered in his name, he is there also (Matthew 18:20). So when we confess to one another, we are confessing to Jesus. But we are also influencing the rest of the body.

According to an early church book, so ingrained was the practice of confessing sin in the first century church that it had become a required part of the corporate, public worship, immediately preceding communion: "In the assembly confess your transgressions, and do not come to your prayer with an evil conscience."[1]

When someone in the early church committed a sin, part of the healing came from telling the others about it. Not just healing for the confessor, but for the rest of the body too. Perhaps because now they had to work through their feelings of self-righteousness. And their desire to judge.

But just as acknowledging our sin is beneficial to the body, so the lack of it can be disastrous. I believe the Holy Spirit is more than passingly familiar with the human tendency to pretend that nothing is wrong when very much is wrong. He knows how we like to hide our evil behavior so we can appear to be better than we are. And he knows how destructive that can be to the body of Christ.

To have Christians with unconfessed sin in our midst who pretend to be holy and godly when they are not inhibits intimacy and trust within the body. On at least one recorded occasion it was also destructive to the sinful believers themselves.

Joseph, among others of the young church in Jerusalem, had set a fine example of sacrificial living by selling a field and giving the money to the apostles for them to administer. His selfless act, his faith, and his love for Christians of lesser means were so highly regarded and so encouraging to the young church that he became known as Barnabas, "Son of Encouragement." He also gained a certain amount of acclaim for his deed.

That acclaim, as well as the high standard which his act of stewardship set, apparently was daunting to those who merely played the church game, who were content only to look the part. Like Ananias and Sapphira. They followed Joseph's lead when they sold their property. But they conspired to keep part of the money for themselves while pretending, in an ostentatious act of charity, to be giving all the proceeds to the church.

Their behavior underscored their lack of faith in the Lord and the power of his Spirit. They trusted in their money, not in

God's grace. And like many of the Pharisees, the ultimate purpose of their giving was to promote the appearance of their own godliness as opposed to the kingdom of God.

Their sin broke faith with the rest of the believers who had everything in common and who shared with one another according to their needs. Can you imagine what would have happened to the faith of the young church had the behavior of these two believers gone unpunished and then become widely known? Cynicism might have run rampant through the body. And instead of following the example of Joseph, other believers might have been seduced to follow the example of Ananias and his wife. They might have become thieves of the riches of God, robbing him of his tithe and bringing a curse on the people instead of God's blessings.

As God had said earlier to his people, "'Will a man rob God? Yet you rob me.

"'But you ask, "How do we rob you?"

"'In tithes and offerings. You are under a curse—the whole nation of you—because you are robbing me. Bring the whole tithe into the storehouse, that there may be food in my house. Test me in this,' says the LORD Almighty, 'and see if I will not throw open the floodgates of heaven and pour out so much blessing that you will not have room enough for it'" (Malachi 3:8–10).

When we are unwilling to confess our sins, unwilling to be vulnerable about our lack of faith, when we desire neither intimacy nor accountability with other Christians, our desire is not to please God. Instead we want to *appear* to please him—and the church—while trusting in powers other than God to preserve us.

Sin infects us like a virus. We sneeze. We cough. Our eyes run. And we say, "Code? Whad code? Dhere's duthing wrong wid be." And in spite of our denial, the sin disease begins to work its way through the body.

No wonder God demanded the lives of Ananias and Sapphira. The wonder to me is that God is so gracious to us today when we behave in similar ways.

A MASK CAN BE A STUMBLING BLOCK TO NONBELIEVERS

Wearing a mask of righteousness is tempting in the body of Christ. It makes us look good in a group where good is so highly valued. But when our masks of righteousness deny that we, like everyone, have sinned and fallen short of the glory of God, they do immeasurable damage to the cause of Christ, not only to those within the body but to those outside as well. I'm convinced that such mask wearing is a satanic scheme to disenfranchise the lost and keep them isolated from a saving knowledge of Jesus.

I recently hired a man to repaint my house. During the job he and I had the chance to talk, and I learned he was a recovering alcoholic. He had been sober for almost six months thanks to Alcoholics Anonymous. Alcohol had cost him his marriage, a relationship with his daughter, his business, and his self-respect. AA, on the other hand, had shown him acceptance and love, talking tough when he needed it but never judging him. I told him that sounded a lot like the church.

He seemed surprised by the comparison. I went on to tell him the church was a hospital for sinners, not a country club for saints. He was amazed—not that I had resorted to such a trite image, but by a concept that was fresh to him.

"I never thought of church like that," he said. "I always thought...uh, you know..."

"That Christians were perfect and only 'good' people went to church?"

He looked sheepish, like a little boy caught drinking out of the milk carton. "Yeah."

"A lot of people believe that. Some church people even believe it. But it's not true. The church at its best is much like AA. People recognize they are sinners and but for God's grace they will become enmeshed again in sin, just as you could be trapped again in your addiction. In fact, AA got its twelve steps right out of the Gospels.

"People go to church because they have been saved from all the rotten things they thought and did. But they are still under construction...kind of like this room. You've got the job and you've been paid some money, but you're not finished yet. I know you are going to do the best job you can, but right now it looks pretty awful with paper taped on the walls, these nasty tarps on the floor, and three different colors of paint all over the place. Sometimes the church can look great from the outside while from the inside it can look as nasty as this room. That's because people continue to make mistakes. But God doesn't hold it against them anymore."

The painter was amazed to hear a church-going Christian say that he made mistakes, that he wasn't perfect. That simple confession had a profound and perhaps lasting impact because what he had seen of Christians was the nice clothes, the shining faces, and the sweet talk. He had never been shown the struggles of the followers of Christ while God is reconstructing us. He had seen judgment but not compassion. He had seen what appeared to him to be perfection, but through the stained glass window he had never seen grace.

CONFESSION IS NOT OPTIONAL

God's grace only works in the presence of sin. Without sin there is no need for grace. When there is sin that we refuse to see, God may provide the catalyst for confession that brings us face to face with our transgressions so his grace can go to work.

Jonah thought he knew better than God what the evil Assyrians of Nineveh needed. They were the godless Gentiles who were responsible for carrying Israel into captivity. So when God told him to preach in Nineveh that they might be saved from their wickedness, Jonah couldn't believe it. Instead, he caught the first boat out to a port in southern Spain, as far as he could go and still be in the civilized world, in hopes of running and hiding from God.

But he couldn't hide from God any better than we can. The Lord pursued him, intent on bringing him to repentance and submission to his divine will. When a raging storm came out of nowhere, the superstitious seamen began casting about for an explanation. Their passenger, asleep in the hold, seemed a likely choice—especially after they cast lots and the Lord showed them that Jonah was the reason for all their problems. Realizing he could no longer hide, Jonah demanded to be thrown overboard in order to save them (Jonah 1:1–2:10).

For the next three days Jonah spent his time thinking and praying and probably holding his breath in the smelly belly of a giant fish. When his prayers went up to God, they were prayers of confession and contrition. They were prayers of repentance. And when the fish burped him out on the beach, Jonah was true to his word before God. He went to Nineveh and delivered the message God had given him.

But it didn't happen until he agreed with God—he confessed—and turned from his rebellious path (Jonah 1:1–3:3).

Peter's confession, while different, was under no less dramatic circumstances. Jesus told Peter that he would deny him three times before the cock crowed twice. And sure enough, in the dark hours before dawn, Peter rejected Christ on three separate occasions, each time more vehemently than the one before. After shouting in anger, "I don't know him!" Peter heard the rooster crow a second time. Peter's and Jesus' eyes met across the courtyard of the high priest's house. In that moment Peter's heart cracked under the weight of his guilt, and he confessed his rejection of Jesus, not through words, but through an anguished look followed by broken-hearted weeping (Luke 22:54–62).

One of the greatest difficulties of mankind is admitting when we have fallen short of God's plan for our lives. When we miss the mark, which is the literal meaning of the Greek word we translate as "sin," we are loathe to admit it. Instead we often would like to pretend that the arrow we released from our bow really did strike the center of the bull's-eye rather than missing the entire target. Sounds foolish, doesn't it? It is. "If we claim to be without sin, we deceive ourselves and the truth is not in us. If we confess our sins, he is faithful and just and will forgive us our sins and purify us from all unrighteousness. If we claim we have not sinned, we make him out to be a liar and his word has no place in our lives" (1 John 1:8–10).

There is a natural inclination to follow our own way instead of God's way. That's what Jonah was doing and that's what Peter did. So did David when he seduced Bathsheba and murdered her husband and his men. He knew what was right and what was wrong. But in choosing to follow his own lusts instead of the leading of God's spirit, he also chose to hide the infamy of his deeds from himself and from others.

Jonah justified his running away by saying the people of Nineveh didn't deserve to be saved. Perhaps Peter justified his betrayal by saying he did deserve to be saved, that he certainly wouldn't be any good to Jesus dead. Yet he hung around, watching Jesus. Waiting. But for what? For an opportunity to act? A chance to take word back to the others? And what would have happened had he agreed with each accuser that he had been with the Galilean preacher? Wouldn't he have lost any opportunity he might have had to be effective? What about David? How did he justify his seduction of Bathsheba? Possibly by reminding himself he was the king and he had worked hard and he deserved it.

Each of these men of God chose their own path over God's. And each would have been doomed by his sin had he not confessed it and repented of it. Each of them was convicted in his heart of the evil he had done. And each, with a contrite heart asked God for forgiveness. David who "was a man after God's heart" called on God to restore him to the way the Lord had intended him to be: "Create in me a pure heart, O God, and renew a steadfast spirit within me" (Psalm 51:10).

Does it seem strange to you that God would honor our confessions? It does to me. Because the heart of humans is deceitful and capable of fooling even the one in whose chest it beats. Sincerity is such a difficult conviction to muster.

Yet sin can either be hidden or acknowledged. Once it is acknowledged, spiritual and emotional healing can begin. Confession is the God-ordained avenue by which we avoid the pit of denial that hides our sins even from ourselves. When my young painter friend introduces himself at an AA meeting, he says, "Hi, my name is Mike. I'm a grateful alcoholic." Alcoholism is a disease of denial. By admitting the fact of his addiction, he can't deny its hold on him.

Sin also is a disease of denial. How refreshing it would be in our churches if we introduced ourselves in the same way. "Hello, my name is Jim. I'm a grateful sinner." So long as we resist confessing our sins, we can pretend they don't exist. Or that they aren't that bad. Or that since God's grace is sufficient and Jesus' blood is constantly washing over us, why bring up yesterday's headlines? Let's just forget it, as God has. You know, put it as far away as the east is from the west. Of course, if we take that popular human tack, we will never learn from our mistakes. And history unlearned is bound to be repeated. On the other hand, once we confess, we can begin to grow in Christ. And the reality of our sinfulness can never be far away. Neither can our need for Jesus.

PAIN MAKES US GROW

My dad used to say that pain makes you grow. The reason is that pain makes us learn. It's a great motivator. We learn more from our mistakes than we do from our successes because human beings are pain avoidant. If something hurts once, we don't want to do it again. That's one reason people find it so difficult to follow diets and exercise programs. The pain makes us want to stop.

And that, of course, is one of the God-planned purposes of pain. Pain is a signal that what is happening is to be avoided. And it doesn't matter whether the pain is physical, emotional, or spiritual. When we feel pain, in whatever realm, our tendency is to back off, stop what we are doing, and try something else.

Emotional and spiritual pain are two of the consequences of sin. Sometimes we can hide from the pain and pretend it isn't there. We can deceive ourselves for years or decades until we actually make our confession. But when the heartfelt confession comes, with it comes the deferred pain. The suddenly released pain can overwhelm us as the reality of what we have done, how we have dishonored God with our redeemed lives, how we have wounded others, becomes real to us.

There is pain. But there is also gain. Because with the pain comes healing.

Confessing anonymously tends to reduce the pain we feel on confession. And so there is a tendency not to benefit as much from our mistakes. A loving God will often force us to come face to face not only with our sin but with the consequences associated with it.

David didn't want to confess his sin with Bathsheba. If he had been allowed his way, no one would have known what had happened. David was content to let everyone think Uriah had sired the child when David had summoned him back to Jerusalem.

But God would not allow his adultery or the murder to remain hidden. When David's sin with Bathsheba was finally uncovered by Nathan, the king's pain was intense and long. Because he confessed, the Lord spared his life, but he did not remove the consequences of David's sin. And so David felt pain, which reinforced his desire to be God's man and never to sin so vilely again.

PAIN NOT PENANCE

Central to the images of confession is the concept of penance— the notion that if I have done wrong I must make up for it by doing something right. At its best, penance flows from a conviction that we have hurt another and we want to make it better. That is what led Zacchaeus to make restitution to those he had harmed with his unjust tax collecting. "But Zacchaeus stood up and said to the Lord, 'Look, Lord! Here and now I give half of my possessions to the poor, and if I have cheated anybody out of anything, I will pay back four times the amount.' Jesus said to him, 'Today salvation has come to this house, because this man, too, is a son of Abraham. For the Son of Man came to seek and to save what was lost'" (Luke 19:8–10).

At its worst, penance is believed to save people. Those who believe this way might use Zacchaeus as proof. "See! Jesus saved him because he gave back what he stole!"

That misses the mark. Restitution may be justice. But it isn't innocence. And Zacchaeus didn't make amends in order to be saved but out of gratitude for his salvation.

The reality is that the little guy with the stone cold heart had an emergency transplant by the Master Physician, which caused him to change his ways. As a tax collector Zacchaeus was treated as unapproachable by the religious leaders. He was anathema and as such was not welcome into the family of Abraham, regardless of his genealogy. Yet Jesus welcomed him with open arms, cleansing him and showing that God accepted him by going to his home for an impromptu dinner party. Jesus accepted him while he was yet a sinner, just as he accepted us while we were still sinners.

After accepting Jesus as Lord and before he gave back what he had extorted, Zacchaeus was wealthy, guilty before man, and forgiven by God. Afterwards he was less wealthy, he was still guilty before man, and he was still forgiven by God. But he knew that. We are the ones who get confused.

It is our confusion—and our desire for innocence—that turns penance, an act intended for grace, into one of legalism. The sinner's goal becomes innocence through atonement. If he can do the "right things," it will be as if the evil deed had never been done. The act of penance loses its significance as an expression of sorrow. Instead, it becomes an act of sufficiency, totally apart from the blood of Jesus. Performing the act is seen as the means to forgiveness, not the sacrifice of Christ.

What a mistake. For it is only Christ's blood which saves us. If anything else could do it, then Jesus' sacrifice was in vain (Galatians 2:21). It is because of their salvation that Christians do good, not in order to be saved. If there is value in penance, it is to demonstrate the repentance of the heart and the gratitude one has for God's forgiveness.

There is another problem with penance as it has developed through the ritual of confession. It is so painless. What does it cost to recite the Lord's Prayer five times? Not much in time. I can say the Lord's Prayer in under eight seconds. And I could shave off a second or two if I tried. But I might never engage my heart. Such an approach to penance is like making your church contribution through a payroll deduction. You never feel it.

There is almost no pain. So there is little growth, little gain. A confession is made, and easy penance takes the place of hard repentance.

SPECIFIC CONFESSION STRENGTHENS THE BELIEVER AND THE CHURCH

Some people think a loving God doesn't want us to open ourselves up to others who might be judgmental of us. But he does. That is one of the strengths of the ritual of confession. It takes at least two to do it. There is the priest, and there is the penitent believer. And where there are two believers, there is also the Author of Forgiveness, the Giver of Grace. They all work together to administer that grace.

We've looked at how confession is done in Catholic churches. But what about the Protestant denominations? In my experience with more conservative, evangelical groups, I've often seen it follow this pattern. At the end of the service the preacher invites all who would confess Jesus as Lord to come forward. He also invites those who are burdened down to come and ask for the prayers of the church. Typically the penitent believer walks down the aisle to the lingering strains of "Just As I Am" or some similar hymn to make a generic confession to the minister or elder, requesting the immediate and ongoing prayers of the congregation.

"Pastor Bob, I have sinned and I need the prayers of the church." Or, "Brother Jones, I'm having a hard time with my temper. Would you pray for me?" Such generic confessions may be quite sincere, but they skirt the core problem. When we confess, let us confess with boldness!

"I yelled at my wife, screamed at the kids, kicked the dog, and punched my fist through the living room wall yesterday. My temper is out of control."

"I succumbed to the temptation to cheat on my income taxes. I lied about the contributions I made to the church."

"I want to trust God with everything—the big decisions as well as the small—but I'm not able to. I keep giving him things and then yanking them back out of his hands."

"I've been having an affair with the woman down the street."

"I overstated my expense account, again."

"I don't trust God to give me my daily bread...or anything else. I want to do everything myself."

These kinds of statements lay our souls bare for our fellow Christians to see...and to minister to. And the effect of confession on people can be profound—among the strongest healing medicines there is.

A man was admitted to a psychiatric hospital in a deep depression and threatening suicide. He had been sexually abused as a child, but what was most distressing to the staff was that he had sexually abused his daughter on a regular basis for several years.

My reaction was probably similar to yours. I felt repugnance and disgust. I had told myself I could work with anyone except an incest perpetrator. Now, here I was, face to face with one, and I was responsible for helping him get better.

For several days the man stayed locked in his shell, hiding behind the walls he had built to protect himself. He smiled. He joked. He commiserated. But these were parts of his mask. His participation was only at a surface level. He rarely revealed anything of consequence about himself except to talk about how others had victimized him.

As the week wore on, he began to expose the hidden parts of his life. The instances of victimization he was willing to disclose became more and more malignant, his descriptions more and more lurid. He told about the lack of nurturing he received as a child. He talked of his father's harsh brutality, his mother's distance. Never did he remember being hugged. No one in his family ever told him, "I love you." With each revelation he became more and more bold because with each revelation he received the same level of acceptance from the staff and his peers. By their love they showed him that what he had been through was both abnormal and terribly painful. And because of their acceptance, he felt safe, perhaps for the first time in his life.

One morning during group therapy he began talking in his usual, detached manner. He spoke unemotionally of the pain he had suffered. After a time tears started to roll down his cheeks. He continued talking, unaware of what was happening. Then he began to weep. And then to sob. Finally the dam broke, and with great gasps and cries he confessed he had molested his daughter.

We all cried along with him. My tears were of both joy and grief. Joy for the lowering of his mask and the invitation of other Christians to come into a private place he had never shown before. Grief for the terrible pain he had experienced and the terrible pain he had caused.

The man improved. His depression lifted. His thoughts of suicide ended. He began to have hope for the future. He talked about one day asking his daughter for her forgiveness and telling her he was sorry, if she would let him.

He was still broken, still not what God had intended him to be. But he was so much more of what the Lord wanted.

It wasn't what he knew, it was who he knew that helped his healing. He was aware long before he came to the hospital that he had sinned. Yet he had never allowed himself to drop his mask and get close to other Christians before. His mask had also kept him isolated from God. When he finally peeked out from behind the mask, God effected his healing through the relationships the Holy Spirit gave him. The Christians God surrounded him with were spiritual doctors who mended and healed, not spiritual surgeons who cut and ran.

Having the accepting ear of a compassionate brother or sister is important for us to find the courage to confess. But when their compassion wanes, or the acceptance is not there, we must remember that the pioneer of our faith has already trod this path. Jesus is our older brother. He sits at the right hand of God as both High Priest and once-and-for-all sacrifice. He offered himself so that those of his brothers and sisters who murdered, raped, lied, committed incest, and led others into slavery would not get what we deserve. Rather, we would get what no one deserves: unconditional love and acceptance and eternal forgiveness.

The shame and pain of confession pales by comparison.

LIFTING THE MASK

1. When you think of "confession," do you see the images presented in this chapter, or does something else come to mind?

2. Has anyone ever confessed wrongdoing to you when you weren't the one who had been wronged? What did you feel? What did you do? What did you say?

3. Have you ever confessed to someone? Was it scary? How did you feel afterwards? Did it affect your relationship with the person to whom you confessed?

4. Have you ever wanted to confess to someone but couldn't? What could that person have done to make it easier for you?

5. How important do you think confessing is to developing the kind of church Christ intended? Why?

6. What do you think of this passage from Proverbs: "He who conceals his sins does not prosper, but whoever confesses and renounces them finds mercy" (28:13)? To what extent is it consistent with your experience?

Chapter 7

Confusion about Confession

"I confess my iniquity; I am troubled by my sin."
Psalm 38:18

"He who guards his lips guards his life, but he who speaks
rashly will come to ruin."
Proverbs 13:3

Before he discovered the Book of Romans, Martin Luther was a dyed-in-the-wool legalist. He was terrified of God. "He could not trust in God as a reconciled Father, as a God of love and mercy, but trembled before him, as a God of wrath, as a consuming fire." He believed that only by not sinning could he go through the gates of heaven. So he observed the minutest details of discipline. "No one surpassed him in prayer, fasting, night watches, self-mortification."[1]

Trouble was, like all human beings, he was always sinning. As a young monk he spent hours in his cell, wailing and praying over his sinful state, trying to achieve a clear conscience. In his spiritual paranoia he buttonholed his fellow priests and confessed almost everything, from blatant misdeeds to secret, dark thoughts. Even the patient priests grew annoyed with his constant confessing. "His confessor once told him, 'Thou art a fool. God is not angry with thee, but thou art angry with God.'"[2]

I get the idea that Luther viewed the route to heaven as a steep, glassy hill, and he was wearing shoes with banana-peel soles. He was afraid even the smallest sin could send him sliding down the slippery slope to eternal damnation. For him, salvation was a fragile thing, more dependent on his behavior than on Christ's sacrifice.

And then he read Romans. Here for the first time his eyes were opened to the majesty of God's grace and the ongoing gift of forgiveness he had through Jesus' blood (Romans 3:20–24). And here ended his ceaseless, neurotic confessing.

Martin Luther continued to struggle with his sinful nature. And he continued to confess his sins to his brothers. But the Lord relieved him of his anxiety. He discovered that confession is agreeing with God that we are sinful, not attempting to save ourselves by becoming perfect.

CONFUSION ABOUT CONFESSION

Perhaps like Luther we also get confused about this thing called confession and view it as an all-or-nothing phenomenon. If we're going to start confessing, do we have to confess everything to everyone? Are Christians to have no secrets, no private thoughts? Not at all. It is no more true than the notion that we must open ourselves up to everyone we know, everyone we meet.

Confession is an act of extreme transparency. In heaven we

will walk around fully knowing and fully being known. But now we live in a fallen world, not paradise. And sometimes prudence demands discretion in what we show the world—or the church.

WHAT SHOULD WE CONFESS?

God values relationships far above all things. He valued relationship with us so much that he was willing to die to assure it. That is why he sent and sacrificed his son for us. So it is that any time we damage a relationship by our sin there is a need for confession to that person. And the closer and more important the relationship, the more pressing the need for confession.

Following this principle, it is vital for me to confess sins that affect my family and sins that affect my Christian family, the church. While a case could be made that all sin affects my family and all sin affects the body of Christ, practically speaking the sins I believe require confession to others are those that most directly impact them.

That is why many of the people of Ephesus, following the demonic drubbing of the seven sons of Sceva, confessed their sins and burned their scrolls on sorcery (Acts 19:13–20). They had been looking for power, but they had not been interested in submitting themselves to God's will to get it. Instead they had focused on the occult, which draws its power from Satan. They heard of the power in Jesus' name and began using it as another magical incantation. It was then that God allowed the demons to attack Sceva's sons.

When the people of the community heard of this, many

became believers. It was important for them to renounce publicly their past involvement with the occult or else the body of Christ would have been weakened. Their confessions signaled a critical turning point in their decision to follow Christ. Afterwards they destroyed property that was worth more than an average person could earn in 130 years. Following such a demonstration of confession and change and commitment, "the word of the Lord spread widely and grew in power" (19:20).

Sins which affect the church include gossip, slander, covetousness, withholding of tithes and offerings, greed, unbridled anger, jealousy, envy, and the creation of strife. Paul lists much more extensive catalogs of such sins in Colossians, Philippians, Ephesians, and the letters to the church at Corinth. All of the sins he mentions cause damage to the church, especially when they go unconfessed. Because unconfessed sin is manifest behavior that is unlikely to change.

Sexual sin and sins of violence against family members must also be confessed. These sins attack the fabric of the family, and so they endanger the very society in which we live. If they remain unconfessed, I believe they maintain their power to hurt.

CONFESSING WHAT WE CAN'T FORGIVE IN OURSELVES

Even when Christians give sins over to God, sometimes they can't get them out of their minds. Like a haunting melody, the memory of the sin and the shame and pain associated with it are unshakable accompaniments to life in general. Obsessing on any sin can give the devil a foothold in our lives and can sap us of the joy God intends.

As far as I can determine, there is no example in the Bible of someone's confessing a sin and then continuing to feel bad about it. David may come closest in the aftermath of his sin with Bathsheba. Some might say Psalms 32 and 51 are a result of his inability to feel forgiven. I don't think so. Rather they seem to accent the grief that comes from a failure to confess, and the joy of restoration of relationship with God that follows the confession.

Never does David say anything resembling what we commonly hear believers—perhaps including ourselves—say: "I know God forgives me, but I just can't seem to forgive myself." When we say that, we are assuming a role and a power that are not ours. Only God can forgive sin. Our job is to accept the forgiveness once it is given.

Temptation to pornography is a kind of sin that often continues to burden down the believer. Some men and women have a secret obsession with pornography that makes them unable to prepare for sexual relations without it. It fills their minds with erotic images, images that are the very essence of lust because they reduce the object of desire to just that. They are no longer human beings with human needs. Rather they are fleshly automatons designed only to give pleasure to the one who peruses them.

Such images can become obsessions that fill the mind. And, as with any addiction, the dose must be increased to maintain the thrill. The images become more blatant, less subtle. The sex less implied, more graphic. Without increasing levels of titillation, arousal is blunted.

God can deliver one from the consequences of such sin, but rehabilitation is rare in a vacuum. The way out is often through confession of the obsession to another person and establishing a relationship of accountability.

Some women—and some men as well—have similar difficulty with images of children they have been responsible for aborting. Though God has forgiven them, either they are unable to accept his forgiveness, or they just can't shake the traumatic images.

At the time of the abortion they may not have fully understood what they were doing—"I didn't know it was a child!" Or they may have been pushed along by the wave of public opinion—"Everything I read, everything I heard said it was OK." Or the decision may have been taken from them by well-meaning parents—"I was only sixteen and my mother made me have the abortion." Or they may have been overcome by fear of discovery or plain, old-fashioned selfishness. Though they now have been saved and God has forgiven them, they can't shake the images of either the abortion or the child that might have been.

One woman I know kept playing the tape in her mind of the horror she felt after her abortion as she looked over at another young woman who had just undergone the same procedure. The woman beside her had blood all over her sheet and gown. "Is that what happened to me?" she kept saying. Another woman marks in her mind each passing birthday of her "son." She wonders what he would have been like. "He would be graduating from high school this year. I wonder if he would have been a good athlete. Or if he would have made good grades." Both women are convicted of the part they played in the death of their children. Yet for years neither was prepared or willing to talk to anyone about it. Talking meant acknowledging the decisions they made, the guilt they had. And that always raises the question, "How could God forgive what I have done?" They had no idea of the answer, and for years they were unwilling to allow anyone else to help them see it.

Now they have chosen to unburden themselves, and healing has begun. Yes, they did participate in the killing of their children. And, yes, God was not pleased. But they are learning that through confession and talking with the right people they are able to be freed from the obsession that has driven their lives for so many years. They are beginning to understand that only God has the capability to forget and forgive the unforgivable—that when he forgives our sins he removes them from himself as far as the east is from the west, and he remembers them no more (Psalm 103:12; Isaiah 43:25). Forever.

When God forgives sins, he forgets them. He wipes them out of the book. It is as if they never occurred. Those are capabilities beyond the scope of any human being.

And they are capabilities God is more than willing to exercise on our behalf. While there is no way to make restitution for some of our sins, the God of all grace forgives us anyway. I think

James had in mind those of us who can't seem to accept God's forgiveness when he said, "Therefore confess your sins to each other and pray for each other so that you may be healed. The prayer of a righteous man is powerful and effective" (James 5:16). After confessing and talking with trusted friends and counselors, even those who have been plagued by memories of abortions are beginning to recognize the magnitude of his forgiveness.

WHEN SHOULD WE CONFESS?

Generally speaking, the more quickly sin is confessed, the better off we are. Unconfessed sin is similar to fish left on the counter. The longer it sits, the stronger it gets.

When sin goes unconfessed, it not only affects the sinner, it can have a profound impact on the one who was injured. The injury can take on a life of its own.

Corrie Ten Boom tells of an encounter she had years after her release from a concentration camp. She was delivering a lecture on forgiveness one evening. The lecture had been well received, and she felt as if the Lord had used her to reach people.

Afterwards an older man approached her and told her he had been one of the guards in her camp. Her reaction surprised her. She, who had just told people how to forgive, found herself not wanting to forgive this man who had hurt her and so many others with his monstrous behavior. She wanted to lash out at him.[3]

Her experience came back to my mind recently when I was also challenged to forgive an old debt.

Twenty years ago, I was wounded deeply by another person. I tried my best to forgive him and move on with my life, but periodic contact would reopen the old wounds. The result for me was a smoldering anger and a growing bitterness. Many times through the two decades I believed I had truly forgiven him only to find a new area of unresolved anger.

A few days ago as I was putting the finishing touches on this manuscript, he called me and asked for a meeting. When we got together, he told me he was there because the Holy Spirit had told him to come. Then he confessed that what he had done over the years had indeed been wrong and was an affront to God. He realized he had hurt me deeply and there was nothing he could do to make it right. All he could do was admit it and ask for my forgiveness.

I couldn't believe it. I truly thought I would go to my grave never hearing those words. I had wanted to hear them many times over the years. But they had never come.

Now I found myself saddled with a strange set of conflicting thoughts and emotions. I was happy he had finally come to see me. I knew it had taken great courage. Confession always does. But I was angry that I didn't feel it would be sporting to grab him by the throat and yell, "You're right! You were wrong!"

So I thanked him for his courage. I told him I forgave him…which I did. And we prayed together.

It would take a while for my emotions to catch up to my intellect, but my intellect had grabbed my will and said, "We will do this. We will be gentle with one another."

Had the confession been made twenty years before, not only would the pain and grief of two decades have been avoided, but so would much of the emotional conflict that followed. Perhaps the bitterness would have dissipated more quickly too.

So when is the best time to confess? Now. Whenever *now* is, that is the time to fall on our knees and tell God what we have done, agreeing with him that we have failed him. Then we must allow him to lead us into appropriate acts of recompense.

A rule which works with relatively healthy people is that when a sin causes us trouble with others, with God, or with ourselves, it's time to confess it. Our lives and relationships with God and with others will improve remarkably.

Without confession, sin and sinners can go underground. The relationship damaged by sin receives further injury because now the sinner wants to isolate from those he or she has wounded. To confront them means confronting the sin and coming face to face with the guilt. For many of us that is a step too painful to take. So we turn the tables, accusing our accuser. Or we avoid the person altogether. We start going to a different church. Or we stop going to church completely. The same dynamic takes place in families.

I know a young woman whose parents divorced when she was in middle school. The father had many affairs during the marriage, and the mother finally divorced him. Shortly after the divorce the angry little girl confronted her father. He responded with name calling and anger of his own, anger directed at the mother but delivered to the daughter. At the end of the confrontation he stormed away from her never to return. The longer he stays away, the more deeply he wounds his child, and the harder it is to return. And so he isolates further.

The desire to isolate is strong when our sins remain unconfessed. Guilt and shame combine to keep us away from those who might confirm our deepest fears—that we are unworthy of anyone's kindness or forgiveness. And, of course, our guilt and shame keep us from those who could help us realize the grace God has for all sinners.

Sometimes our sin can harm us emotionally, causing us to feel depressed, sad, or anxious. It can also interfere with our sleep. Debbie Bailey, one of my prayer partners, believes that wee-hour awakenings are the work of the Holy Spirit, arousing us to pray. I like that explanation better than mine: I always figured it was simple anxiety. When I do what Debbie suggests, when I pray for the person on my mind or the situation at hand, the anxiety often evaporates and I quickly go back to sleep.

At other times, when the catalyst awakening me is unconfessed sin, the only path to peace is confession. So when I am able to act with wisdom, I find someone to confess to as soon as the day begins in earnest. The next night my sleep is likely to be undisturbed.

TO WHOM SHOULD WE CONFESS?

So to whom should we confess?

First, to God. The most common Greek word we translate as "confess" is *homologeo*, which means "to agree with." The implication when referring to sin is that God already knows our transgressions and he holds us accountable for them. Only when we agree with him that what we have done is a violation of his will can we begin the process of repentance. That is what makes confession so hard. We already know God doesn't like what we have done. And we can bet others won't like it either.

Second, if our behavior has caused us trouble with another person, it is usually best to confess to him or her. It's the flip side of the principle Jesus gives on how to maintain relationships in the church. In Matthew 18:15 he says if our brother has something against us we are to go to him and talk it over. I think he assumes that if we have wronged our brother we will naturally take care of whatever problems we have caused by going to our brother and talking about it.

Finally, we can confess to one of our fellow priests, another Christian. I believe this should be someone within our closer circles of intimacy: a good friend, a respected family member, or an elder or minister with whom we have a trusting relationship.

When I confess sin, I don't lightly choose to whom I will reveal myself. I don't sit down with the church directory and a random number table and see whose name comes up next on the list. Nor do I bare my soul each time before the entire congregation.

The person to hear our confession is someone with whom we already have a respectful, loving relationship, someone who honors Jesus as Lord and who takes that relationship seriously, someone we can trust, someone who has godly wisdom.

TO WHOM SHOULD WE NOT CONFESS?

I would offer one further warning about confession. Confession to someone we have wronged should never be made only to make ourselves feel better. When we have hurt others, whether they know it or not, and our confession will only cause them deeper pain while relieving us of guilt feelings, my rule is don't confess to them. In situations like this we must work out our confession with other Christians and with God himself.

Let me give an example. A man marries a woman who is pregnant, but not with his child. The man loves the woman and is willing to forgive her and to parent the child as if the child were his own. After they are married, the woman becomes pregnant by her husband. Now the husband feels conflict; he feels more love for his natural child than for the child his wife was carrying when they married. He keeps quiet about it until the child is a teenager.

At that point he feels he can no longer live a lie, so he takes his adopted child aside and confesses that he is not his father. He also acknowledges to the teenager his feelings and asks the teenager's forgiveness for his inability to love him as much as he loves his sibling.

Has he done the right thing? Absolutely not. He chose to be that child's father regardless of the biological parentage. That he begins to feel differently towards his adopted child later has nothing to do with the child and everything to do with the man's own psychological processes.

In a case like this, confessing to God may be adequate for his emotional healing. He may also need to share his sin with another. He may need counseling. But anything he says to the child will only create wounds from which the child may never recover.

If we find ourselves burdened with guilt, confessing to God may release us from that guilt. Or we may need to share our sin with another. If we are unclear about what to do, we need to pray. And have confidence. The Lord will help us know what to do, and with whom.

LIFTING THE MASK

1. Do you relate more to Luther before he "discovered" the Book of Romans or after? In what ways?

2. What do you think of the concept of *homologeo*, the Greek word we translate as *confess*, meaning to agree with what God already knows to be true?

3. What advice would you give someone who had committed a sin for which he or she did not feel forgiven?

4. Is confessing sooner rather than later always better? Can you think of a situation when it might be better to wait to confess to someone?

5. Does confessing to a fellow believer relieve you of the responsibility to confess to God? Why do you think so?

6. When, if ever, should you not confess to someone you have wronged?

Chapter 8

Healed by the Body

"My guilt has overwhelmed me like a burden to heavy to bear."
Psalm 38:4

I knew something was dreadfully wrong the instant he strode into my office. His body looked rigid, as if a steel rod had replaced his spine. Or as if he had been dipped in wax and allowed to cool. The slightest movement threatened first to crack, then to shatter, his entire being.

He sat in the offered chair, making meaningless small talk. He was looking at the wall beyond me. Then he did it. He confessed. It was simple and to the point.

"I did a bad thing."

Over the next hour he unraveled the ball of string that was his life, between sobs and tears and blowing his nose. He talked of his sin, committed years before, which he had never divulged to another human being except the one he had wounded. As he talked, the wax did crack, but his being wasn't shattered. It was freed. The energy he had used for self-protection was released for healing.

He had prayed on many occasions. He had given his burden to Jesus, and he had been forgiven. And he had made restitution, much as Zacchaeus had done. At least three times over he had paid for his sins. But it didn't feel like enough. He had the need to confess to another person.

He was right. He had done a bad thing. A very bad thing. It was the sort of thing that causes pain in the moment and keeps on causing pain in the future. The actual sin is not important for our discussion. What is important is that he had carried the burden of his offense for years.

Other people might carry their sins in public, but no one knew of this man's sin. His was secret sin, cordoned off, kept in darkness, hidden far away from the eyes of mankind. And in the darkness it festered, purulent and toxic.

So why after all this time did the man feel the need to confess? And why to me? He had confessed to the one he had wounded. He had confessed to Jesus. Why did he need to confess to someone else?

I can offer three possibilities.

THE NEED FOR SUPPORT, NOT CONDEMNATION

Sin can cut us off at the knees. Once we recognize the impact our sins have had on ourselves or on others, we can be overwhelmed.

We need someone to help hold us up. We need support, especially as we try to reverse our previous course and live right. "Brothers, if someone is caught in a sin, you who are spiritual should restore him gently.... Carry each other's burdens, and in this way you will fulfill the law of Christ" (Galatians 6:1–2).

The man was weighed down by a tremendous burden that

had become so heavy he could barely shoulder it anymore. He needed someone to help him with it. That's why he came to me. At the very least he wanted to be able to talk with another person about the pain, the disappointment, the fears.

In my office hangs a poster with words attributed to Anne Sullivan, Helen Keller's teacher. It says: "Children need guidance and sympathy far more than instruction."

These are wise words for the church also, as we attempt to bear one another's burdens. The children of God need love and respect, guidance and sympathy more than they need condemnation. "For God did not send his Son into the world to condemn the world, but to save the world through him" (John 3:17). If the Son of God did not come to condemn, who are we to assume that role in his name?[1]

One of the important and unique functions of the church is to encourage one another. When others "gently restore" us, their love encourages us, they help us feel safe, and we become bold enough to drop our masks. Condemnation and judgment just shove the masks on tighter.

Our guilt weighs us down with the constant accusation that we are not worthy to be in the presence of others as we are. When others listen to us and accept us, their love and acceptance expose that lie and lift the burden from our shoulders.

THE FALSE NEED TO FORGIVE SELF

Another reason he needed to confess to another person was that he had not yet forgiven himself. Oh, in his head he believed he was forgiven. But the transgression was so great he had continued to see its effects on both himself and the one he had wronged. The rupture sin caused in their relationship remained. In fact, even though he had confessed to the one he had wronged and had taken steps of restitution, little relationship was left. While some healing had occurred, it was incomplete. The wound was still raw.

Satan, the Usurper, the author of sin, was whispering in the man's ear. Satan, who longs to take the role of creator, creates nothing but destruction. When he whispers in our ears that God's forgiveness is not enough, that we need to forgive ourselves, he leads us into usurping God's role, as he did.

We sin. We ask God for forgiveness. He forgives. But we don't accept it because we don't believe that what we have done can really be forgiven without more pain and suffering on our part. So we compound the original sin by taking forgiveness out of God's hands and assuming that responsibility ourselves. The logic is rather insane, isn't it?

THE REAL NEED TO FEEL FORGIVEN

But if we can screw up the courage to risk removing the mask in front of a trusted Christian brother or sister, we can see the acceptance of God acted out by his people. We no longer feel as if we haven't been forgiven because we can see God's forgiveness mirrored in the way they behave towards us.

When we fail to accept what we see, it is often because of the shame we feel, that sense of not being good enough. At its root, shame is an ophthalmological disorder. It is basically "I" trouble.

The focus is on self, and so long as self remains the focus, we cannot be fully Christ-centered.

When the man chose to unburden himself with me, he was really attempting to shift the focus, whether he knew it or not. He wanted to see if I would run away from him once he told me the horrible thing he had done. He had been watching me for some time, listening to my Sunday school teaching, observing how I related to other people. He had talked with me about different subjects. He wanted to know if I was safe because he was looking for someone with whom to take a terrible risk. He yearned to expose his sin, yet he wanted to minimize the chance of rejection and judgment. So he watched. He observed. He waited. And then he walked in and said, "I have done a bad thing."

Can you imagine the courage it took to say those six simple words? With "I have done a bad thing" he let the mask drop. And once it dropped, he could never replace it with me. He could never go back to his place of isolation so far as he and I were concerned. He was exposing himself in a way that would not allow his focus to remain on himself. It now included me as well.

THE PRIEST IS STRENGTHENED TOO

This powerful act of confession involves more than the repentant sinner. It involves the priest who hears the confession too. Intimacy is never a one-way street.

And intimacy is not without pain. Both of us felt pain that

day. He, the pain of uncovering; me, the pain of knowing. And there was no quick remedy for either.

The man told me terrible secrets. They weren't my secrets, they were his. So they were secrets I could never entrust to another human being. Loving him would mean holding them, perhaps for a lifetime.

I was appalled. I was revolted. I was angry. I wished I had not been chosen for such duty. It hurt to look at such things. I realized there were human behaviors I didn't want to see up close and personal. There were things I didn't want to know about this person, things I didn't want to hear. I knew that once I heard them I could never unhear them. They would always be a part of me. Now having heard such things, how would I relate to him in the future? Would I shrink in disgust or anger whenever I saw him?

The righteous parent in me wanted to jump up and down and shout in his face, "How could you...?" It wanted to sit in judgment and say, "Didn't you know the pain you would cause?"

But he knew. He knew the depths of his sin and its effects on the other person far better than I ever would. He knew it from the inside out. He didn't come to me to hear that he was wrong.

As he continued the awful confession and pushed on in his anguish, I began to suspend my judgment and my righteous indignation. My compassion grew, and my heart began to ache for him. I wanted to weep with him. I longed to reassure him, to tell him everything would be all right. Because as he talked, I began to realize the depth of his losses, the extent of his alienation. I saw the pain that could drive a man to such sin.

I'm so thankful God didn't want me to be his judge. I was to be his confessor, his priest. I was to be the mirror that reflected his value and worth, regardless of what he had done. I was to be Jesus to him.

As he talked, I also began to see something more. I pegged the author of his pain. It was the Old Man.

CONFESSION DEFEATS THE ACCUSER

Satan was behind the whole thing, from start to finish. Satan was behind the sin. And Satan was behind the self-imposed exile that had kept this man from meaningful relationships for so long. For years the fear of discovery had kept him moving from place to place, never having a home.

Yet, in revealing his sin to me, the man had defeated his Accuser. After all, how can the Accuser continue to accuse us of that which we have confessed? The only reason any accusation has power is if we have to pretend we are not what we are. Once we acknowledge we are sinners, where is his power to hurt us? The power of Satan comes in his convincing us never to tell.

Satan would have us never tell another soul of our sin, to maintain a portion of ourselves in eternal isolation, creating a dark hell inside to which we have consigned a part of ourselves. Even though we confess to God, even though we confess to the one we have wounded, we feel we must hide our sin from everyone else lest they reject the badness, and us with it.

But in confessing the man had cemented a relationship with another believer that would outlast the shame of his sin. He was continuing the process of dismantling the wall that had kept him alone and isolated. That process began with his confession to Jesus, and it was advanced with his confession to me.

He had relinquished the need for self-forgiveness. He had sought and gained the prayerful support of the church. He had seen Christ's love and acceptance in the body. Now, with his mask pulled back a little, his healing could continue. And he no longer felt the need to run. He had found a place to call home.

LIFTING THE MASK

1. How have Christians helped you carry your burdens?

2. Is forgiving oneself a biblical concept? How would you explain your answer?

3. Have you ever been called on to hear the confession of another Christian? What was that like? What emotions did you experience? How did you benefit?

4. Have you ever thought about confession defeating the one who accuses? How is Satan, the great Accuser, defeated by our confessions to one another?

Chapter 9

The Fragile Bridge of Trust

"Like a bad tooth or a lame foot is reliance on the unfaithful in times of trouble." Proverbs 25:19

When we choose one of our fellow Christians to be the priest for our confessions, there are others, many others, we will necessarily exclude. They won't be brought into our confidence. And from their perspective we might appear to be cold and closed, unwilling or even unable to share our true selves.

That's okay.

Because trusting everyone can be as destructive as trusting no one. It can even be worse. People may not appreciate our openness. In fact, they may use it to hurt us, either on purpose or by accident.

Revealing our innermost thoughts and passions to everyone without regard to who they are is self-destructive. It is living life without boundaries, and life without boundaries is life that is unsafe.

Everyone is not worthy of our trust. Perhaps not even all the members of our families. Or our churches.

Remember the man who confessed to me he had done a bad thing? He had grown up in a family whose members were not trustworthy. He had also married women who weren't. He had chosen business partners who looked and behaved like those unsafe family members. So it was hard for him to know what a safe, healthy relationship looked like. When he had dared to drop his mask in the past, he had often been attacked by those who professed to love him. By the time he decided he needed a confessor, he had learned caution. That's why he observed me for so long before he risked confessing to me the evil he had committed.

A friend of mine also grew up in a terribly destructive family. Her parents and other caregivers betrayed her over and over, violating emotional and physical boundaries at will. They showed little respect for her. She existed to serve their needs, not vice-versa. When she made the mistake of being vulnerable with them, they would often turn on her, using her feelings and secrets to hurt her.

That presents quite a dilemma, doesn't it? How can we know when it's safe to let others see behind our masks? How do we know when it's OK to be transparent?

FUNCTIONAL SYSTEMS
MAKE MASKS UNNECESSARY

One of the fundamental purposes of all functional systems—church, family, or otherwise—is to provide safety for their members. With safety the individual members can risk being transparent with one another. These healthy systems have at least three things in common. They respect each other. There is honest and open communication between members. And individual members can trust one another.

It's hard to say which should come first. Each feeds the others. We will be more willing to trust others if their communication is honest and open and if they respect us. If, on the other hand, they are closed and guarded with their communication or they are unwilling to trust us or show respect for us, we will not be very willing to be vulnerable to them.

When any one of the three is missing, fear and uncertainty enter the picture, and transparency becomes clouded. Masks are created to provide the safety that is missing from the system.

RESPECT

I think few Christians understand the implications of this for the church. Take the issue of submission for instance. In one of the most misapplied passages in Scripture, Paul says wives are to be submissive to their husbands (Ephesians 5:22). Men and women have battled over the meaning of this verse in their attempts to exercise power and control over one another and to avoid responsibility for their behavior. The result has been a lack of trust, guarded communication, and loss of respect.

Paul uses the same Greek word—*hupotassos*—for *submit* that Luke used when he described Jesus' obedience to his parents (Luke 2:51). He used the same word to describe the new relationship God ordained between the angelic and demonic powers and his son in Ephesians 1:19–21: "And God placed all things under his feet."

In all these instances *hupotassos* means to put oneself under the authority of someone else, to obey. That was all right for Jesus as a boy. Mary and Joseph were good parents. And Jesus is responsible and respectful of the forces placed under his authority. But the history of men exercising that same respect and responsibility towards submissive women is not so consistent.

I believe that's because we ignore both the umbrella passage and the real meaning behind the word *submit*. The overarching passage is Ephesians 5:21: "Submit to one another out of reverence for Christ." Here *hupotassos* describes the relationship of all believers to each other.

God calls us to love and respect one another. One way that manifests itself is through giving way, submitting to each other. If we place ourselves in mutual submission to each other, then we will not find ourselves guilty of lording it over one another. Respect and love will not allow such behavior. Instead we give way in an effort to provide what is best for the other person, rather than fulfilling our own selfish agenda. That's what love is—wanting what is best for the other person. And this is how the world will know we are his disciples—if we love one another.

Respectful, submitting love implies vulnerability, just as Jesus was vulnerable. God delegated all power in heaven and in earth to his Son, yet when occasion demanded, Jesus held his power in abeyance. He did so with Mary and Joseph. At the age of twelve, on the cusp of Jewish manhood, out of respect for his parents and the culture and his heavenly Father's wishes, he chose to remain under his parents' authority for another eighteen years. Out of respect for God and the work of John the Baptist, he allowed John to immerse him in the Jordan (Matthew 3:13–17). And he certainly withheld his power in Gethsemane and on the cross. He never quit being who he was. But he did choose to submit to others out of respect for them or out of respect for the One who sent him.

OPEN COMMUNICATION PAVES THE WAY FOR TRANSPARENCY

Trust and safety can also come when we can see forgiveness in practice and in the honest transparency of another.

Shortly after my problem with graduate school became a dominate cloud over my life, I was scheduled to speak at a singles ministry conference in another city. Before the conference began in earnest, the six other singles ministers and I gathered to get to know each other better.

I had decided on the flight up that it would really be great if I could drop my mask with these guys. If I didn't, because of all I had been going through, it would be obvious I was holding something back. But I didn't know them very well. Some I didn't know at all. Others I only saw once every twelve to eighteen months. I was afraid if I let them hear about my school trials and my own misgivings about ministry that instead of being an "innie" I would become an "outie." And being an outsider is no fun. I feared if they saw what was really going on in my life and how frustrated I was they wouldn't want me to be a part of them.

But God wanted me to talk. He wanted me to risk being vulnerable. That's why he had me sit next to Kevin Stewart.

On the way to our meeting place we all rode in one van. My seat mate was Kevin, a fellow I had never heard of before, let alone met. Yet it turned out Kevin had been best friends with the deceased husband of one of the single women at Oak Hills, a woman I had known for years.

We chatted for a few minutes, and then Kevin took the conversation to a deeper level. He decided to drop his guard and speak openly about his journey into ministry. As he talked, I kept thinking about the apostle Paul telling someone he used to murder Christians.

Kevin is a former drug dealer. He was reared in the church, but somewhere along the way things fell apart and he turned his back on it. He began dealing and using cocaine.

Kevin talked of his addiction both to the drug and to the money being a dealer provided. And he talked about how God had pulled him out of that sordid world and put him on a path to ministry. Then he asked how things were going with me and my ministry.

My first impulse was to give him a "Fine, thank you" and change the subject. That would have been easy, but incredibly dishonest. And it would have been cowardly and disrespectful after Kevin had been so forthcoming. So for a brief moment a small battle raged inside me. Should I trust this guy, or would he trample my confidences if I laid them at his feet?

After a pregnant pause I made a decision. It was obvious he had allowed Jesus to transform him. Jesus had become his Lord. I wanted to talk about what had been happening to me, and God had given me someone safe to talk to. I would have been foolish not to seize the opportunity.

I started by telling Kevin about my decision to get into ministry and then my need for further training. That led to talking about my frustrations at school. I told him how burned out I was and how I had misgivings about continuing in ministry. I even told him about wanting to run off to Alaska or Tahiti.

Kevin listened with compassion and respect. His acceptance of me, warts and all, helped me to trust him further, and that trust began to spread to the rest of the group.

About that time we arrived at our destination. We piled out of the van with snow falling like a silent shroud all around us. It had turned suddenly cold for the month of March, and the late snowstorm caught everyone by surprise, including the weather forecasters.

Once inside we found quiet respite in the warmth of the living room. The house belonged to the parents of one of our number, and his mother had all sorts of goodies ready for us: fresh, homemade cookies, hot tea, coffee, hot chocolate. It was like one of those perfect family scenes from a 1950s television program. I half expected Lassie to come bounding into the room followed by Timmy and June Lockhart. Only this was real life.

After we got settled, introductions began. When my turn came, I picked up where Kevin and I had left off. I laid out the whole tale, including my own shortcomings. The other men proved as worthy of trust as Kevin had. And they did more. They lowered their own masks. They asked questions, expressed sympathy, and shared some of their own stories of frustration with higher education. They spoke of their own struggles with ministry and how hard sometimes it is to follow the dreams God has given us. Then we prayed for each other.

When I had stepped into the van with the other men, I felt capable of keeping only my minimal obligations. I would deliver the lecture I had prepared. I would be sociable and friendly. But that was it. When we started, I didn't feel I belonged, more because of my own hurts and doubts than a lack of confidence in what I had to share. Before we were done, I felt a bond with these men I had rarely felt before. And the catalyst was Kevin's transparency. His frankness and his willingness to be open and to be changed by God allowed me to trust enough to communicate openly, first with him, then with the others. As I laid the valuables of my heart before them, they proved to be loving brothers of Jesus.

TRUST

Trust is like a bridge built from pebbles and assembled without cement. It is hard to build and easy to break. Trust built over years can be broken in an instant. Almost any parent knows that to be true. So do those who have had a loved one betray them.

After the affair, or after the child has violated important

family rules, or after the friend has betrayed us, the common question is how will we ever trust again?

Indeed.

We know that living behind a barricade of protection is as isolating as it is secure. We long to trust others. It is the way we were created. Yet how do we learn to trust when trust has once—or many times—been betrayed?

The answer is the same way porcupines make love...very carefully.

My friend who had been reared in a destructive family wrestled mightily with trust. As she became an adult, she decided she needed counseling to get beyond her childhood losses.

As she scouted out available therapists, one professional kept being recommended to her as someone who was well suited to help. She talked to people who had been his clients. She arranged to be involved with him in community service projects and professional groups. She watched him from a safe distance to see how he related to others. She watched his heart. She saw how he respected others, how he trusted them, and how open and honest his communication was. And on occasion she extended a small piece of herself to see how he received it. Like the servant in Christ's parable, if he proved trustworthy in the little things, she would consider entrusting larger things to him (Matthew 25:14–21).

Slowly, over a period of two or three years, she had enough trust pebbles in place to build a bridge between the two of them.

And so she took the final risk of entering a therapeutic relationship with him.

Not everyone is so wounded or has had their trust betrayed as much or as often as this woman. And not every situation requires establishing a relationship with a professional therapist. But a case could be made that all trusting relationships are corrective relationships, relationships that help us heal from prior wounds.

Professional relationship or personal, the process of building trust is the same. Sometimes it happens more quickly, as it did with Kevin and me. Sometimes it takes longer, as with my friend and the counselor. As time passes, people expose a bit more of the important parts of themselves, and they find that instead of running from conflict, they can stay and resolve it.

Somewhere along the way they learn they can safely pull out the treasures of their hearts and lay them at the feet of their friend, trusting the friend to receive them with honesty and love and respect. Just like Jesus.

LIFTING THE MASK

1. How hard is it for most people to trust? How hard is it for you to trust?

2. Describe a time when your trust was violated.

3. What do you do to overcome your fear of trusting people?

4. In your opinion, how important is trust to being transparent? How about respect? How does honest, open communication relate to trust and respect?

5. Is there someone with whom you would like to establish a greater trust relationship? What steps would you take in building that bridge?

Chapter 10

We, the Priests:

A High Calling for Lowly People

"You also, like living stones, are being built into a spiritual house to be a holy priesthood, offering spiritual sacrifices acceptable to God through Jesus Christ." 1 Peter 2:5

"Each one should use whatever gift he has received to serve others, faithfully administering God's grace in its various forms." 1 Peter 4:10

Throughout the book we have been talking about the role of the priest in hearing confessions, in interceding, in offering prayers and petitions on behalf of other Christians. But exactly who is that priest?

You are. Me too.

No kidding. It's true.

It doesn't matter how old we are. Or how young. It doesn't matter whether we are career-minded businesswomen or stay-at-home house husbands, cleat-eating, football-playing boys or cheerleading, braces-and-lipstick girls. It doesn't matter whether we are married or single, divorced or widowed. As long as we have been born again in Jesus Christ, we are priests of God Most High.

Jesus himself was a priest, which is unusual since all the priests of Israel hailed from the tribe of Levi. God had ordained that only those from the line of Moses' brother, Aaron, could serve as priests in Israel. Yet Jesus, like David, was from the tribe of Judah. And his priestly order predated that of Aaron.

Jesus was a priest after the order of Melchizedek.

THE ORDER OF MELCHIZEDEK

Melchizedek—it's a name shrouded in mystery. He was the priest-king of Salem, the fortress city on whose ruins Jerusalem was built. His name means "king of righteousness," and his title as king of Salem means "king of peace." Both foreshadow Jesus, the king of glory, the son of righteousness, the prince of peace.

As our older brother and our advocate, Jesus intercedes on our behalf with the Father. And that, of course, is the original and historical role of priests: to be intermediaries between God and mankind. That is what "intercede" means—"to stand between." Jesus, our great high priest who is always before the throne, stands between us and God. Because he has been one of us, he can tell the Father what it is like, how difficult the temp- tations are to resist, how much it hurts sometimes to be human, what loneliness is like. It is this intercession, coming to the Father on our behalf, that Jesus lives for. It is how he saves us (Hebrews 7:25). His blood is a continual sacrifice, cleansing us from sin and making us acceptable to God.

Going to bat for us is what Jesus does. And that is what a

priest does. When we pray before God for each other, we are administering God's grace, just as Jesus does.

ADMINISTRATORS OF GOD'S GRACE

Most people know when they have done wrong. They really do. They pretend they don't know because it gets them off the hook, momentarily. Many of the masks we wear are our attempts to avoid acknowledging the truth, either to ourselves or to others. But people really do know. And they know God knows. What they don't know is how to get out of the mess they are in.

That's where you and I come in as God's priests.

Originally priests offered sacrifices on the altar, and God provided the fire which consumed them (Leviticus 9:24). The priests were given the task of keeping it burning (Leviticus 6:13). Born-again believers, the new priests of God, have been given a fire in their breasts. The Holy Spirit blazes within us, filling our bodies, his temple, with God's presence, just as he filled the tabernacle with his presence when the children of Israel offered their sacrifices. We have also been given the task of keeping the sacred fire burning within us. The New International Version literally says, "Do not put out the Spirit's fire" (1 Thessalonians 5:19). Is it any wonder that God's priests are warned not to put out the fire of the very Spirit that empowers them to administer God's grace in this world?

When people learn I'm a minister, they often ask how many other ministers we have on staff. It's a trick question. Or rather it's a question that begs for a trick answer. Because what they want to know is how many paid staff ministers we have. But the answer to the question is there are over twelve hundred ministers at the Oak Hills church. Because all of us—paid staff included—strongly believe that every member of the body of Christ is a priest, devoted to administering God's grace to the world.

An obvious example took place just five minutes ago.

Last night someone drove a car through the garage door of the home of one of our single parents. On purpose. The culprit tore it to smithereens and badly damaged her car which was inside. Then he drove away, tires screeching in the night. It terrified the woman.

Rose is more fortunate than many single moms whose husbands have left them with the debts and responsibilities of child rearing while taking with them most of the earning capacity. Rose is a professional, a licensed vocational nurse. What she earns is adequate to her needs…if she budgets carefully. But Rose hasn't been able to plan for this kind of contingency. Willful vandalism is not a line item in her monthly budget.

Nor has Rose planned emotionally for such a disaster. Who has? If someone drives a car through your garage door at four o'clock in the morning and then runs off, you might feel violated, raped. It's scary. And it can stay with you for a long time.

What if whoever did the deed decides to come back? What if that person is furthering a vendetta against some family member by attacking the house? The night before it was a brick through the front window. Last night a car through the garage door. What can she expect next? Bullets? Homemade bombs?

Early this morning Rose called one of the other single women in our home Bible study, our Life Group, to tell her what had happened and to ask her to pray for her. The woman did pray, interceding for her and asking for God to protect her and give her courage and wisdom. Then the woman started calling other members of the Life Group.

That evening some of the other "priests" met at Rose's house and prayed some more. Then they served her further by helping clean up the mess, feeding her and her children dinner, and gathering personal items so they could spend a few nights at another single parent's home.

All of those people were using the gifts God had given them to administer his grace to Rose and her family. They were all serving, following the example of Christ who came not to be served but rather to serve (Matthew 20:28). They didn't need a professional to tell them what to do or how to do it. They only needed to love a woman and her family and minister to them the way they would want to be ministered to. Service is the essence of ministry, and it is at the heart of being a priest.

As priests we offer sacrifices of prayer and forgiveness on behalf of others. We bring the good news of God's forgiveness to those who have sinned. We serve others. And we make the conscious decision to forego any retribution that might be due us when we have been wronged. We sacrifice our "right" to vengeance.

When we become priests, we don't have to go out and buy a potato sack and make a hooded bathrobe so we can look the part. Nor do we have to develop a brogue like Father Flanagan or look piously down our noses at those who are not so holy as me and thee. You can be a priest wearing what you're wearing right now and talking just as you talk right now. And you can administer grace in those same clothes. Or grander ones. Or the ones you use to work on your car or weed the flower beds. Or you can do it in hardly any clothes at all, like the native Guarani Indians of South America.

PRIESTS COME IN ALL VARIETIES

The year is 1760. The Guarani Indians inhabit an idyllic setting in the wilds of South America. Their lands are above a mighty cataract rivaling Niagara in size. Only two routes lead to their village. One is through the dense rain forest. The other is up the sheer rock walls of the waterfall. These natural barriers have kept them safe from the Old World invaders. Until now.

Two very different men have found their way to the domain of the Guarani. Father Gabriel is a Jesuit priest, intent on teaching the Indians the gospel of liberty. Rodrigo Mendoza is a mercenary, intent on trapping the Guarani and selling them into slavery. Those he can't capture he shoots with his long flintlock rifle.

Both are men of faith. Gabriel's faith lies in God. He has given himself to the establishment of a mission in a wild and hostile world. Mendoza is a cultural Christian, reared in the beliefs of his parents but never having encountered the living Christ. His faith is in his sharp eye, his strong arm, and his hard heart. He hides behind his macho ruthlessness. If any man has ever been in need of a priest, Rodrigo Mendoza is such a man.

After a brutal foray into the jungle the mercenary returns to the city. But he fails to find the solace and relaxation one might equate with home and civilization. Instead he discovers his wife in bed with another man—his own brother.

Mendoza struggles with his rage and his sense of betrayal. He does not want to harm his brother, yet the fires of his anger flare with the slightest provocation. He is not able to stop the inevitable.

Meeting his brother in the town square, the mercenary's passion ignites, and he kills the younger, unarmed man with his sword. Appalled at what he has done and overcome with guilt, Mendoza gravitates to the local cloister. He spends the next six months overwhelmed by depression, loss, and self-loathing. He has murdered his brother. For that he knows there can never be forgiveness.

Meanwhile Father Gabriel has been converting the Guarani, establishing a mission in their village. On his return to the city the priest is asked to visit the monastery where Mendoza has been staying and minister to the distraught killer.

The priest makes his way to a Spartan, open cell in which an unkempt man sits, motionless, silent. Mendoza is certain God will not forgive him for his sins. How could he? Mendoza cannot forgive himself. Nor would he forgive the deed had it been committed by another. He knows nothing of forgiveness. All he knows is retribution.

Father Gabriel tries to make contact. "What you have done is bad. What you are doing is worse."

After several moments Mendoza's haunted eyes look up, and he snarls, "There is no redemption for me, Father!"

"There is forgiveness for all sin," replies the priest.

"I am a mercenary. I kill for money."

"Will you dare to do the penance of your choice?"

"Will you dare to see it fail?" challenges Mendoza.

Neither the priest nor Mendoza understands God's grace. They believe the sinner has to do something to make up for the evil he has committed, as if somehow he can save himself. Gabriel tries to administer God's grace through penance. Mendoza believes that same penance will fail. But they are both off base. Jesus' sacrifice is sufficient without any further sacrifices from either Mendoza or the priest. Jesus' blood even covers fratricide and slavery. But Mendoza and Father Gabriel don't know that. So the two of them construct an elaborate penance for Mendoza to perform.

Accompanied by four grieving priests, Mendoza returns to the watery canyon before the falls that protect the Guarani homeland. He drags with him a great net filled with heavy iron armor and weapons, the tools of his accursed trade. He has been pulling this tremendous burden for days and miles, since they left the city. Rodrigo Mendoza's clothes are in tatters, his long, black hair sodden and stringy with perspiration and dirt. His face is soiled, his hands bleeding. Each step is agony, not just for Mendoza, but for the compassionate priests who accompany him as well. This burden is the penance he has chosen. It symbolizes the life he wants to turn away from. How long he will drag it, how far, is unknown to both priests and penitent.

Suddenly the netting catches on a rock outcropping, and Rodrigo's progress is halted. He strains against the inch-thick ropes, trying to break his burden free. His feet grapple for purchase, but he slips and falls to his knees. Still he pulls against the ropes, but he can pull until his heart bursts, and he will never be free.

Unable to stand the futility of Mendoza's position any longer, a priest cuts the rope and releases the man of his burden. Mendoza falls face first into the river mud. For a moment he lies there. Then he raises his head and shoots a look of condemnation at the priest. He is not ready to be released. Acting as his own god, he has decided there is still more to be done before salvation can be found. Without a word he picks himself up, goes back, collects his cargo of shame, reties the rope, and resumes his journey. With tears in their eyes and prayers on their lips, the priests continue with him.

Soon they reach the base of the waterfall and begin the perilous ascent. It is a difficult climb unburdened. With the awkward, unbalancing weight of the armor dragging behind, it seems impossible. Rodrigo Mendoza's strength is pushed to the limit. The cascading water thunders around and over him as, rock by rock, he ascends the cliff face. Still he struggles upward, focused on his own pain, his own agony, oblivious to the compassion of his priestly escort.

At last, exhausted and covered with mud, Mendoza wrestles his body and his burden over the top of the cliff. On hands and knees, head down, he pants in the safety of the flat beside the river.

Waiting for him are the fierce Guarani, their faces and half-naked bodies covered with paint. These are Father Gabriel's converts, but they look more like bloodthirsty savages than born-again Christians.

The Indians have been watching the party make the long, painful ascent up the waterfall. And they have recognized the man dragging the armor. He is the one who cracks the air with thunder from the long stick, sending blood and death through the jungle. Grief and fear transform Father Gabriel's face as one of the young warriors, his features hidden behind a mask of paint, draws his razor-sharp long-knife and grabs the exhausted Rodrigo, who is still on his knees, by his filthy hair.

The warrior harangues him in an unknown tongue, shaking the man's head and waving the knife. Rodrigo Mendoza waits in resigned patience for the edge of the blade to give him release. He seems to long for it.

But both the priest and the mercenary mistake the passion of the savage. The Guarani warrior thrusts the long blade forward, sliding it beneath the rope on Rodrigo's back, and slices upward, severing the rope and releasing the burden of armor and weapons. With disgust he kicks the heavy net and its contents over the edge into the water far below.

Could it be that the new convert has understood what neither the priest nor the penitent have: that the blood of Jesus is always enough, no matter what the sin? This half-naked savage will be forgiven much in the Kingdom to come, for he has forgiven his brother Mendoza much. He has given his burdened brother in Christ what Mendoza was not able to give his own flesh-and-blood brother. He has forgiven him completely. And, more. He recoils before the one who has grown up in the culture of Christ. It is as if the savage understands the incongruity of the affront Mendoza's attempt at penance is before the God of all grace. To this new believer in Jesus, the burden of armor is Mendoza's failure to accept Christ's forgiveness. It is more disgusting than is the one who carries it, the one who has killed his Guarani brothers.

Realization breaks slowly over the face of the humbled mercenary. The knife has released him, but not as he expected. His burden has been taken away, his sin forgiven. And in a most surprising way.

Mendoza's mask begins to crumble. No longer can he sustain the pride that has kept all the priests at bay. He weeps. He wails. He sobs. The wounded man starving for salvation emerges from the penitent bent on saving himself. And the Guarani warrior stands beside him, his hand brushing the ex-slaver's face in a gesture of comfort and acceptance. And forgiveness.[1]

Like Jesus, he has looked on his tormentor with compassion.

Like Jesus, he has waived his opportunity for retribution, sacrificed his right to vengeance, and forgiven his persecutor. Like Jesus, the Guarani has become a priest of God Most High after the order of Melchizedek. Like Jesus, he has administered God's grace.

It is not likely we will ever have the opportunity to spare the life of someone who has murdered our own brother. But we will frequently have the opportunity to serve others in love. We will be able to pray with them and for them. And on occasion we will be privileged to stand in the breach before God on behalf of people who have been so beaten up by the world, so deceived by the Father of Lies, that they will believe that for them there is no salvation. And we, like our Guarani brother so many years ago, will make a profound difference in the life of another human being. Because we too are priests of God Most High.

LIFTING THE MASK

1. What does it mean to you that Jesus was a priest after the order of Melchizedek?

2. Do you think of the kind of help the Life Group gave Rose as "priestly"? What priestly functions did they perform?

3. Why does it sometimes happen that those who administer God's grace most effectively are not the professional ministers but the "rank and file" priests?

4. Read 1 Peter 2:9. Do you agree that the Guarani warrior was a priest? Do you think of yourself as a priest of God Most High? In what ways?

5. How does receiving God's grace administered by one of God's priests allow people to lower their masks?

6. How does viewing yourself as a priest change the way you look at your life? What new responsibilities do you see for yourself? How can you administer God's grace in your everyday life?

Chapter 11

How to Lift the Masks

"And we urge you, brothers,...encourage the timid, help the weak, be patient with everyone." 1 Thessalonians 5:14

We all wear masks. I do. You do. And that person over there does too. Sometimes we know they are there. Sometimes we don't.

Our masks are often unconscious creations, donned and held in place by forces outside our conscious control. They pop up during times of distress and go away, if at all, during times of safety.

As a result, we rarely see our own masks. Others might be able to. And God always can. But we are largely blind to them. Trying to see our own masks is like looking in a mirror and trying to see our eyes move. We need help.

That doesn't mean we don't catch glimpses of our masks from time to time. And we may realize that it would be best if we worked to get rid of them. But if we are not sure they are there, if we are not aware of the extent to which we have camouflaged ourselves, then we will need help in learning about them.

WHAT HELPS MOST

One way we help is when we are transparent with each other. When we are transparent with others, we build trust. When we are transparent, we cannot remain strangers. We come to know each other, and we trust what we know.

There's a chicken-and-egg problem here though. Because for us to be transparent requires trust. And how can we trust others without perceiving transparency in them? It's a circle of logic that has no beginning and no end. If we are going to help, we can either jump in with transparency or we can jump in with trust.

So which comes first?

I believe it's the trust. But not our trust of others. Our trust of God. The more we are able to trust God, the more we will be willing to be transparent with other Christians. God's perfect love drives out fear because perfect love is utterly trustworthy. We will be willing to look inside ourselves to the extent that we recognize the safety and love we have with our Father.

As we follow the greatest commandment to love the Lord our God with all our heart, soul, and mind and then the second commandment to love our neighbor as ourselves, we will have trusting, transparent relationships. When we love others, we are being Jesus to them. No one is safer than the bringer of grace, the one who demonstrates God's love.

WITH LOVE COMES RESPONSIBILITY

However, our love for others also demands that we respect their unwillingness to see within themselves. They may not be ready.

There may be masks of which they have caught glimpses that they are not willing to look at further, right now. We must respect that and love them anyway. If they experience our love, some day they may be willing to look more deeply. We don't know what wounds have helped to create their masks. It would be rude and invasive to force them to look at something they are not ready to see. It could even be destructive.

WE MUST FEEL SAFE

In essence, our job in helping others see behind their masks is to be a loving container for them. The more we love and accept others for who they are, the safer they become. And the safer they feel, the less need they have for defense mechanisms like masks.

They will feel safe when they are sure we will not gossip about them. How devastating it is to hear what we have shared in unguarded moments being discussed by others.

They also need to experience as much unconditional love as we can muster. It may be that they will venture to confess some truly unpleasant deeds to us. They may tell about a lapse in faith. Or how they negotiated a business deal in a dishonest manner. Or how they were betrayed in love. Or their role in an abortion. We may be horrified and disgusted at the deeds. But we must continue to love and accept them to the best of our ability. If we pray for that level of acceptance, God will give it to us.

Rarely do others need us to tell them that what they have done is wrong. They know that. What they need to hear from us and see in us is our willingness to stand beside them as they let us see behind the mask, just a little. That will encourage them to drop the mask even more.

As we become transparent with them and share with them the joys and woes of our own lives, the more unconditional trust they can place in us, the more valuable they will feel.

Practically speaking, when we are transparent with others it is often in spite of our fears. Sometimes we feel a need for extra insurance, so we may say things that seem incongruent with a trusting, loving relationship, like "Promise you won't hate me," or "This is just between you and me." While these are often unspoken rules in a friendship, sometimes I think it helps people to feel safe if they get them out in the open early on.

THE CHURCH PROVIDES
CORRECTIVE RELATIONSHIPS

In Christ's church you and I have a corrective relationship. Corrective relationships are those that help remedy deficiencies we have had in past relationships. They can be with best friends or teachers or loving aunts and uncles and grandparents and spouses. The church at its best provides these kinds of healing relationships through love, acceptance, encouragement, gentle exhortation, and accountability. When Christians behave in these godly ways, we are always encouraged.

To encourage is the opposite of dis-courage, to take someone's courage away. When we encourage others, we fill them with boldness. Paul asked the church at Ephesus to pray for him so that he might speak fearlessly (Ephesians 6:19–20). Paul afraid to speak? That's not a trait I associate with such a great lion of a Christian. But he needed the prayers of the church in order to be filled with courage. If that is true for Paul, is it any surprise that others need our prayers and acts of encouragement too? "Therefore encourage one another and build each other up, just as in fact you are doing.... And we urge you, brothers,...encourage the timid, help the weak, be patient with everyone" (1 Thessalonians 5:11–14).

Our patience and encouragement can make a mighty eagle of a tiny sparrow. And then we can soar together to the heights God has planned for us as a church.

PRAY FOR THEM

Pray for the people behind the masks. Nothing is more powerful than prayer. Pray for them without ceasing. Pray for them when you go to bed and when you awaken in the morning.

And we should pray when we are together. In my office one morning Max Lucado said, "Wouldn't it be great if Christians prayed at every parting? Not a long prayer but a simple prayer of thanksgiving and encouragement." We try to do that among the staff at Oak Hills. And it is tremendously encouraging. It helps us stay focused.

I try to pray with everyone who comes into my office. The effects can be profound. People often break into tears and sobs as we pray. I have found that the more armored they are, the more wounds they have suffered. And the more wounded they are, the less likely they will be to pray without help. The goal is for each of us to be an independent and fervent pray-er. When we pray with others, we help them toward that goal.

SO THEY CAN PRAY FOR THEMSELVES

Sometimes people cannot pray for themselves. Sometimes the burdens and losses of life weigh so heavily that they have to have someone else intercede for them, as I did. Yet they cannot have a healing relationship with God without prayer of their own. It must be frequent and fervent, focused and intense. The more they talk with God, the more they will want to talk with him, and the more they pray, the more they will reveal about themselves. That happens with every relationship we develop, so it makes sense it also happens as we develop a relationship with the Father.

Paul told the church at Ephesus to "pray in the Spirit on all occasions with all kinds of prayers and requests. With this in mind, be alert and always keep on praying for all the saints" (Ephesians 6:18). That is my goal, to pray in the Spirit on all occasions with all kinds of prayers and requests.

It lifts me up to know that I can talk to God about anything. I don't just have to come to him with holy requests or holy language. I can sit with him and tell him about the frustrations of house-breaking my puppy. I can tell him how anxious I get when I run out of money on Wednesday night before I get paid on Friday afternoon. I can tell him how attracted I was to that woman at the church party last Saturday night and how I don't want to be. I can tell him my fears about being attacked spiritually. I can confess my irritation with my constantly breaking car. I can ask him about my decision to change the carpet in my house or my desire to redo the bathroom. These are things I might talk to you about if we were close. Paul encourages me to talk about even such things with the One who knows the number of hairs on my head.

SEEK WISE COUNSEL

In the past when troubles arose, I would burst into action. Typical man. Shoot first, ask questions later. I was the pioneer American, pulling myself up by my bootstraps, the ultimate in independence.

God may admire individual initiative, but there is much encouragement in his Word to proceed only in the context of faithful counsel. Proverbs says, "Plans fail for lack of counsel, but with many advisers they succeed" (15:22). "Make plans by seeking advice; if you wage war, obtain guidance" (20:18). It was difficult for me to seek the counsel of wise people because that meant I would have to tell them the problem I was having. And that meant dropping my mask.

I needed people I could trust, but I also needed those who would shoot straight with me, even telling me things I didn't want to hear. So I developed a personal strategy that might work for others as well. My first step is to do a reality check with those I believe will agree with me. That is the easiest part. But then I include among my counselors men and women whose positions I am less able to predict but whose godliness and wisdom I respect. Sometimes they are elders, sometimes they are Christian business people, sometimes they are women who are great prayers, sometimes they are ministers.

Often as I am sharing the situation for which I am seeking counsel, I find myself hesitant to provide details. My shields are up and I have to override them manually. But first I have to make a decision: do I tell the whole story, or do I hide some facts I feel uncomfortable about? Of course hiding won't allow my counselors to give me their best advice. I have realized that if I really need their input, I will be cheating myself if I don't come clean and spill the whole story.

As we are called on to be one of these wise counselors Proverbs refers to, we need to remember how much courage it can take for a Christian brother or sister to come to us. We need to develop a response that is at once gentle and tough minded, cunning as serpents and gentle as doves.

GOD IS THE ULTIMATE COUNSELOR

While it is wise to seek the counsel of godly men and women, it is wiser still to seek directly the counsel of God. He is to be praised for giving us the wisest and most available of counselors. "And I will ask the Father, and he will give you another Counselor to be with you forever—the Spirit of Truth.... But the Counselor, the Holy Spirit, whom the Father will send in my name, will teach you all things and will remind you of everything I have said to you" (John 14:16, 26).

In times of stress prayer is to be our first reaction, not the last. Rather than hanging our heads and saying, "Well, there's nothing more I can do. I guess we ought to...pray," how much better to say at the outset with hopeful expectation, "I'm not sure what we can do. Let's pray and see what God says."

As Jehoshaphat said to the king of Israel, "First seek the counsel of the LORD" (1 Kings 22:5). The Lord promises, "I will instruct you and teach you in the way you should go; I will counsel you and watch over you" (Psalm 32:8). "Counsel and sound judgment are mine; I have understanding and power" (Proverbs 8:14).

God is the ultimate counselor. He is the source of all wisdom and knowledge and power. He reveals himself through his Spirit and through his Word. "Your statutes are my delight; they are my counselors" (Psalm 119:24). The study we do, searching the Scriptures, provides us with great insight into ourselves and into humanity as a whole.

While God may lead us to human counselors or advisers, they are of little use if they do not acknowledge his sovereignty. God is the one who sees the entire Johari Window of our lives. He is the one who knows all the masks and all that they hide. And he loves us perfectly, accepts us unconditionally, never ridicules us, never tells tales about us.

He has chosen to work largely through the body of his Son. That is how we have come to know each other. Jesus is the common ground we share. Together we are the body of Christ.

It is in the church that we can find our closest friends. It is in the church that we are most intimately involved in the lives of others. We can belong to home Bible study groups. We can participate in Bible classes at the building. We can be involved in praise and worship with the entire body on Sunday mornings. We can experience healing and counsel in small groups and in the private times we spend with individuals in the body. There is no better place for us to learn to drop our masks than in the safety and sanctity of the body of Christ.

Yet, just because we are believers, just because we follow Jesus doesn't mean we can automatically overcome that intense desire to cover up. In the next chapter we will look at the lives of two men who walked similar paths but ended up at two very different destinations.

LIFTING THE MASK

1. Does it seem to you that masks are more conscious or unconscious? To what extent do we have control over them? To what extent do they just happen?

2. How willing are you to risk being transparent in order to help others remove their masks?

3. What does seeking wise counsel have to do with lowering our masks?

4. What can others do to more effectively help you drop your masks? How can you help them?

5. If God is the ultimate counselor, why would there ever be a need to seek the advice and counsel of other Christians?

Chapter 12

Judas and Peter:

When Apostles Wear Masks

"While he was still speaking a crowd came up, and the man who was called Judas, one of the Twelve, was leading them. He approached Jesus to kiss him, but Jesus asked him, 'Judas, are you betraying the Son of Man with a kiss?'" Luke 22:47–48

"Then he began to call down curses on himself and he swore to them, 'I don't know the man!' Immediately a rooster crowed. Then Peter remembered the word Jesus had spoken: 'Before the rooster crows, you will disown me three times.' And he went outside and wept bitterly." Matthew 26:74–75

Ask a hundred people to name their favorite apostle, the one they most want to be like, and you can bet one name won't be mentioned.

Judas.

Nobody likes Judas.

His name has become an epithet to describe a betrayer: "You Judas!" Judas goat is the unflattering moniker given to the goat who leads all the other blindly trusting followers into the killing pens.

Yet Judas was handpicked by Jesus, the only non-Galilean

among the twelve. For three years he was at Jesus' side, observing the master, watching him heal the sick and drive out demons. He was in Nain when Jesus raised the dead son of the widow. And he was there when Jesus shouted, "Lazarus! Come out!" Judas witnessed the deliverance of the demoniac of the Gadarenes and the helter-skelter death of the herd of pigs as they plunged headlong into the great lake. Along with the other eleven apostles he distributed the fish and the loaves and helped to collect the twelve baskets of leftovers, probably eleven and a half baskets more than they started with.

And when the apostles went out in pairs, Judas was among them. Jesus delegated his authority to Judas as surely as he did to Levi or Peter or James. Judas, to whom money was so important, set out with no money, no staff, no extra clothes, relying only on the Holy Spirit. He and his comrade went from town to town preaching the Good News. In addition they freed the captives of demons, disease, and perhaps even death, just as Jesus did.

Yet Judas was never what he seemed.

He was saved, a member of the inner circle, his sins cleansed. Yet he didn't so much fall away as he dived headlong into the murky waters away from Jesus. He turned his back and ran for all he was worth in the opposite direction. And even when he became aware of the evil he had done, he chose not to turn again to Jesus.

JUDAS'S TRAGIC FLAW

So what made him go bad? What could have made one who had once been enlightened, who had tasted the heavenly gift, who had shared in the Holy Spirit, who had tasted the goodness of the word of God and the powers of the coming age…what could have made him turn away from all that?

His tragic flaw was not political zeal or a desire for power. His flaw was simple greed. He was filled with covetousness. That's why he was so upset when Mary used the half-liter of perfumed ointment to anoint Jesus' feet. Like the avaricious manager of a budding star, he wanted his cut, even though he might have to steal to get it. His craving for more led him to steal from the money bag he kept for the band (John 12:5–6).

Matthew says he asked the Jewish leaders for money in exchange for betraying Jesus. "'What are you willing to give me if I hand him over to you?' So they counted out for him thirty silver coins" (Matthew 26:15). For betraying the Son of God, greedy old Judas settled for the price of a slave.

It would seem nobody really knew Judas. To whom was he close? Which of the twelve did he call "friend"? What did his circles of intimacy look like? Had he ever confessed his greed, or was it only in retrospect that John realized Judas was a thief (John 12:6)?

Never is there a conversation recorded where Judas took Jesus or one of the apostles aside and said, "I don't think I should keep the money bag any longer. I have used it for my own purposes, and I can't seem to resist the temptation."

Instead Judas actively covered his actions with a mask of piety. "Why wasn't this perfume sold and the money given to the poor?" he asked when the nard was poured on Jesus' feet (John 12:5).

You can almost see him looking down his nose as he asked the question.

Was he really concerned with the welfare of the poor, or did he just want to stuff the cash register? Some biblical apologists have tried to present him as a man motivated by his vision of the conquering Messiah, but Scripture implies that he acted out of less pure motives. John reports he was spiteful over the wasteful nard episode. And of course he wanted to enrich himself. Matthew reports his sell-out conversation with the priests. Look for political zeal or messianic visions here, and you'll never find them. "'What are you willing to give me if I hand him over to you?' So they counted out for him thirty silver coins."

I don't think he wished Jesus harm, because when he learned that Jesus was condemned, he was flooded with remorse. He didn't want the man to die! Somehow Judas must have thought Jesus would emerge victorious. When he didn't, the betrayer returned to the high priest and attempted to withdraw his charges. He repented of bearing false witness against an innocent man.

He tried to give back the money. But those perverse priests who were supposed to sacrifice for another's sin abdicated their God-given duty. They refused to help him. "What is that to us? That's your responsibility" (Matthew 27:4). And they left him to twist in the wind.

Judas had been with Jesus for three years, yet he had only given intellectual assent to him being God's Messiah, the one sent to redeem sinful mankind from sin. Otherwise instead of going to the temple he would have gone to the cross.

WHAT IF JUDAS HAD CONFESSED TO JESUS?

Can you imagine what the scene at the cross might have been? Jesus is hanging between the two thieves. Mary, John, and the other disciples are standing in a group nearby, their eyes nailed to their Savior. The Roman soldiers are casting lots for the condemned man's seamless cloak. Suddenly, out of nowhere, the betrayer appears. With tears streaming down his face he muscles his way through the crowd. Breaking through, he runs to the foot of the cross, falls to his knees, his tortured face pleading to Jesus.

Mary and John look at each other, aghast. The Roman soldiers step forward. Jesus looks down.

"Forgive me, Lord!" Judas cries.

What would Jesus have done?

I think he would have done what he does when you and I come to the cross today and plead, "Forgive me, Lord!" He would have forgiven him. And Judas, instead of being the one born to damnation, would have been the prodigal crying, "Forgive me, Father, for I have sinned against heaven and against you!"

But it didn't happen that way.

Instead he went to the priests to whom he had betrayed Jesus and confessed. With that he denied the power and authority of Christ. In his remorse he saw no way out. His focus was on himself, not on Christ. Even if he thought about Jesus, his shame over his sin would not allow him to become transparent and beg Jesus' forgiveness. So, engulfed in his misery, he threw the money back into the temple, slipped away, and hanged himself.

PETER, THE CRUMBLING ROCK

How different was Peter, another of many who betrayed Jesus that night.

Old Rocky could always talk a good fight. "I'm with you, Jesus. I don't know about these other guys, but you can sure count on me. I won't ever let you down."

And to his credit, when the bad guys came for his Lord, Peter was the only one who raised arms in Christ's defense. As the vigilantes closed in on Jesus, Peter drew his sword and with a single swipe cut off the ear of a man named Malchus, a servant of the high priest.

I wonder what Peter felt? Elation? Fear? Anger? Hope?

And then Jesus did that miraculous thing that only John talks about. He healed the ear of the high priest's servant as if it had never been injured. And he rebuked Peter and the others, forbidding them to use their weapons. Then he went with his captors. Willingly!

What were Peter's thoughts? "This isn't the way it's supposed to be, Lord! I know you said turn the other cheek, but they're going to kill you! And anybody they can arrest with you! Why don't you resist? Why don't you fight? Call down your angels, Lord! Destroy these enemies of yours! No. Don't let them take you. If they take you, what will happen when they come for us?"

Thaddaeus ran. So did Bartholomew. So did Peter and John. They were afraid for their lives. John Mark followed for a while, but when the men grabbed for him, he was so scared he left them holding his clothes as he ran naked into the darkness.

Somewhere along the way Peter and John found each other. They hung back, watching the hostile mob push Jesus back into Jerusalem, back into the maw of the sleeping city.

The two men trailed at a distance, just beyond the torchlight of the gaggle of Jews. Once again they slogged across the Kidron, entering the city through the Water Gate. If they could only keep themselves out of the clutches of the angry priests, they might be able to rescue Jesus. Perhaps the priests wanted only to question him. Maybe then they would release him.

The crowd took Jesus to the home of Caiaphas, the high priest. John followed them into the courtyard while Peter remained outside. John was well known to Caiaphas and his household, so he had no difficulty getting in. After assessing the situation, he returned and spoke to the servant girl watching the door, while motioning to Peter (John 18:15–16).

"It's okay. I'll vouch for him."

PETER BETRAYS JESUS

Peter was still afraid he would be recognized and arrested, even as he huddled around the fire with the soldiers. So when the servant girl asked, "Aren't you one of his disciples?" Peter's desire for safety overrode his loyalty to Christ. He pretended not to be what he was.

"I am not," he said.

Awhile later he was recognized by another girl as one of Jesus' disciples. Again the Rock denied knowing Jesus, this time more forcefully.

Then he was recognized by a relative of Malchus. "You were with him in the olive garden. Your accent's like his too."

Matthew reports Peter's response to this third attempt to see behind the false front he had put forth: "Then he began to call down curses on himself and he swore to them, 'I don't know the man!'" (Matthew 26:74).

Immediately a rooster crowed and the lights went on for Peter. Jesus had told him he would deny knowing him, not once but three times before the rooster crowed in the dawn. And he had.

At that moment his eyes locked onto Jesus' across the courtyard. Jesus' eyes must have seen to the core of Peter's soul. And Peter couldn't bear to be seen so baldly. He jerked his head away, breaking the momentary connection, and ran off into the darkness. There he began to wail loudly, his body wracked with violent sobs of grief and remorse.

Peter betrayed Jesus as surely as Judas did. Judas did it for money, Peter to save his hide. Perhaps there were higher motives, but we certainly know of the low ones. Both men had pretended to be what they weren't. Yet Judas was damned, and Peter was saved and went on to become a pillar in the church.

SO WHAT'S THE DIFFERENCE?

Luke says "the Lord turned and looked straight at Peter" after he denied him the last time (Luke 22:61). The Greek word used here for *look* is *emblepo* which means "to discern clearly." Jesus saw through the mask Peter had erected with such haste. I believe it was the act of being seen that cut Peter to the heart. Jesus saw Peter's weakness before it happened, and he saw it now as Peter was denying him. No wonder Peter wailed and cried with such violence! He was laid bare with no place to hide.

Peter the Rock came face to face with his own sin, with his own evil. Judas ran from his all the way to his death. He looked on his soul and couldn't bear what he saw. Nor could he bear the thought of Jesus seeing him in the way he saw Peter, the way he saw everyone! So he begged corrupt priests for forgiveness that could only come from the Lord of Life.

Judas didn't become the betrayer overnight. He didn't wake up one morning and say, "I think I'll go sell out the Messiah today." His betrayal was part of a process that gave Satan a foothold from which to operate. Judas was a thief. He was a breaker of confidences. He indulged himself at the expense of others.

And he was a liar. He pretended to be Jesus' friend, ate bread with him, traveled with him. And then sold him out for a pittance. The tragedy is that Judas probably came to believe that the mask he wore was the real Judas. He probably believed he was one of the devoted inner circle, even while stealing from them and betraying their trust. No one believes he is evil. We may recognize we have done wrong, but evil? No way! Evil always describes someone else. That's what rationalization is all about.

So the evil is done then covered with a mask. The mask is the lie. Lies give Satan a foothold from which to influence people for greater and greater evil. Perhaps it was Judas' lying spirit that allowed Satan such a free reign with him.

"Then Satan entered Judas, called Iscariot, one of the Twelve. And Judas went to the chief priests and the officers of the temple guard and discussed with them how he might betray Jesus" (Luke 22:3–4).

With the lies come justification and rationalization. These are often lies themselves. The businessman turns in his expense account and says to himself, "It's okay. They don't pay me nearly what I am worth." The wife cuddles up to the husband of another woman and sighs, "My husband never listens to me the way you do." He responds with, "My wife doesn't understand me."

The lies become a beachhead from which Satan can launch his attacks. Unhindered, he wreaks incredible havoc on our lives.

But we are not powerless pawns. We don't lose our free will when we allow the devil to influence us. We don't become mindless automatons controlled from the pits of hell.

James says, "Resist the devil and he will flee from you" (4:7). The opposite is just as true. Don't resist him, and he will enfold you in his unloving arms.

Judas became the betrayer a little bit at a time. One decision led to another, each lie building on the previous one. He succumbed to greed in the small things, and greed came to own him in the end.

Judas was a thief; Peter wasn't. It seems the lower left pane of Peter's Johari Window—the part that is open to others—was large while Judas's was small. Although Peter failed to live up to his words, he was the same person in public as he was in private. Judas was a different person behind closed doors. But I believe there was one other difference between Peter and Judas.

It was John.

CIRCLES OF INTIMACY

John observed all that happened. He stood with Peter by the fire, warming himself on that bitter morning when the Rock began to crumble. John witnessed each confrontation and each lying response. And he was there in the courtyard as Peter's eyes met Jesus'.

After Peter escaped into the darkness, I believe John went to him, not as the Son of Thunder but as the disciple whom Jesus loved. I believe John, who wrote so much about love, loved his friend Peter as Jesus had taught him. I believe he exemplified the principle Paul spoke of when he said, "Brothers, if someone is caught in a sin, you who are spiritual should restore him gently" (Galatians 6:1).

After the denials Peter needed a friend, someone he was close to, someone who would listen. John could have been that friend. They were so close, had done so much together with Jesus. He would have understood. He experienced all of it with him.

Peter was transparent to Jesus in the courtyard. He could no longer cover up. There was no place to hide. But he could access the power of Christ to help him overcome his shame and his guilt. His friends helped him. And he became like Jesus.

Judas needed friends, too. But there was no one to whom he chose to unburden himself. His only friend had been nailed to a cross.

No wonder no one wants to be like Judas.

LIFTING THE MASK

1. Of these three men—Peter, Judas, and John—whom do you most identify with? Why?

2. What do you think Judas' circles of intimacy looked like? What about Peter's?

3. How might things have been different if one of the disciples had found Judas after he left the money in the temple?

4. What kept him from confessing at the foot of the cross?

5. Why was his confession to the priests not adequate?

6. Which people within your circles of intimacy would you like to get to know better? With which ones would you like to establish a more trusting, accountable relationship? What are the first steps you would take in building those relationships?

Chapter 13

The Body Transparent

"And let us consider how we may spur one another on toward love and good deeds. Let us not give up meeting together, as some are in the habit of doing, but let us encourage one another....
Remember those earlier days after you had received the light, when you stood your ground in a great contest in the face of suffering. Sometimes you were publicly exposed to insult and persecution; at other times you stood side by side with those who were so treated. You sympathized with those in prison and joyfully accepted the confiscation of your property, because you knew that you yourselves had better and lasting possessions."
Hebrews 10:24–25, 32–34

It's been over twenty years since that December Sunday when I walked to the front of the church and risked telling about my dying marriage. That may have been my first major experiment with transparency. It didn't save the marriage. But it set ripples in motion that are still affecting my life.

The divorce was traumatic. To deal with it I sought counseling. People who haven't experienced counseling cannot really appreciate how much courage it takes to do therapy. It is one of the most vulnerable experiences a person can have, leaving you with few secrets unexposed.

During my counseling I learned skills that most of us should know but often don't. I learned that love and acceptance can take many different forms. One is them is active listening—really hearing what someone else is saying. Another is suspending judgment. Another is how to bear the discomfort of being seen, truly seen, by another human being.

Still later I learned the value of family meetings. We all sit around the table, each with his or her own agenda items. Everyone gets to speak, and when anyone is speaking, everybody else listens. As the kids have grown older, we have rotated the chairmanship responsibilities, giving both of them, as well as Mary and me, the opportunity to guide the discussion. These meetings teach leadership. They teach followership They teach respect. And they require transparency and trust.

When a problem is weighing on me so heavily it disrupts the way I work with my family, I am quick now to let the children know I'm having a hard time with some things (the details are usually not important) and that if I seem distracted or strange it has absolutely nothing to do with them. They usually nod or say OK and continue what they're doing, but inside they feel relief because they know that no matter how strained my behavior may be it is not their fault.

When we pray together at night, they often pray about these things. Or they tell me things they need help with, and I pray for them.

Our family is not perfect in its ability to have open and honest communication, trust, and respect, but we do a much better job than we used to. As a result everyone feels safe. Even when Mary and I argue and exchange angry words, as all married couples do from time to time, the kids feel safe because they have learned that transparency is not always sharing quietly and that sometimes intense emotions get in the way of even the best intentions. They know their mother and father will work things out. We will pray. And God will protect us.

Do we wear masks at home? Almost never.

Do we wear masks when we are with others? Of course. I have confessed my own vulnerability to the sin of self-protection. And I'm sure it will continue, in spite of my best intentions. In spite of my best efforts to use everything the Holy Spirit has taught me in this ministry he has guided me into, I still sometimes revert to my old behavior.

Just last night I was leading one of our Singles Core Group meetings. We were having a good time making plans for the Singles Ministry. As the meeting progressed, more and more questions were asked about things for which I didn't have answers. I began to feel anxious...uncomfortable...guilty. I hemmed. I hawed. I tried to look competent. Finally I realized I was doing a dance of self-protection and my mask was slipping into place, so I stopped.

I confessed I had dropped the ball. In fact I had dropped a number of balls. I didn't realize until I began telling my friends what was going on how overwhelmed I felt by the unusual constellation of stressors that were bearing down on me. As I opened up to them and accepted my failed responsibility, as I became more transparent, my head became clearer. I could actually see better, as if the mask had been impairing my vision.

Once they understood the problems, the group was able to combine their resources to help solve them. And they prayed for me. Then the isolation I had begun to feel as my mistakes were revealed vanished.

Scriptural injunctions are so simple, their implementation so hard. "Resist the devil and he will flee from you." "Don't forsake the assembly." "Share one another's burdens." Yet when we trust one another enough to be truly open, when we grasp that we are each priests of God Most High, empowered by the blood of Jesus to intercede on behalf of others, when we understand the value of the body of Christ, then things start happening. When we fail to heed those same teachings, things fall apart.

Imagine for a moment that you have decided to go for a walk. You reach down and put on your shoes, tie the laces, and start walking. Before you've gone very far, your feet start to hurt like crazy. You can hardly walk. In pain you look for a place to sit down. You pull your shoes and socks off and discover a plastic coating that looks like your skin. Curious, you peel it back to reveal terrible sores and blisters and infections.

"What in the world?" you exclaim.

To your amazement a tiny voice comes from your right foot.

"We're sorry. We were afraid. We thought the hands wouldn't like us if they saw what was wrong with us."

A silly example? Probably. But that's what it can be like for the body of Christ when we wear masks, when we pretend to be functioning at top capacity and we're just barely limping along. The body assumes everything is fine, that we need no attention, so it depends on us.

And if the hands are wearing masks to look like ears for instance, and the knees are trying to look like happy spleens, the body will quickly lose its ability to function as a body. The individual members will feel cut off, disenfranchised, and maybe even no longer part of the body at all.

MY WISH FOR YOU

We are the body of Christ, you and I. If people on this earth will ever see Jesus, they will see him in us. We are Jesus to them.

Short of heaven I don't believe it is possible for human beings to live without masks. Our environment is far too hostile and unpredictable. There are too many people waiting to take advantage of us, to gain emotionally or economically at our expense.

But the transparent life can be quite heavenly. And the more we strive to be like our Master, the more we allow others in the church to see us as we really are, the stronger the church will grow, and the more it will be what God intended: a place of comfort and encouragement for those called out from the world.

My wish for you is that you will begin to look behind your own masks and help others see behind theirs. I hope you will recognize the strength you have in your circles of intimacy. And that you will work to shrink the size of the lower left frame of your Johari Window, minimizing the information you keep hidden. Practice honest and open communication. Practice trust. And give respect to all people, for we are each fearfully and wonderfully made. Find someone to whom you can confess both need and sin. Learn what the Bible has to say about your role as a priest of God.

And don't take your eyes off Jesus, the pioneer of our faith. He blazed these trails before us, revealing himself without pretense. He was the one who rent the veil separating us from God, and he can help you remove the veils that separate you from your brothers and sisters in Christ so his grace can be administered (Hebrews 10:19–21).

"For we do not have a high priest who is unable to sympathize with our weaknesses, but we have one who has been tempted in every way, just as we are—yet was without sin. Let us then approach the throne of grace with confidence, so that we may receive mercy and find grace to help us in our time of need" (Hebrews 4:15–16).

NOTES

Chapter 4: Where Do Masks Come From?

1. Rhonda's name and identity and other life examples have been altered for reasons of confidentiality.

Chapter 6: The Power of Confession

1. Everett Ferguson, *Early Christians Speak: Faith and Life in the First Three Centuries*, rev. ed. (Abilene, Tex.: ACU Press, 1987), 181, 184.

Chapter 7: Confusion about Confession

1. Philip Schaff, *History of the Christian Church*, vol. vii (Grand Rapids, Mich.: William B. Eerdmans Publishing Company, 1910), 115–19.

2. Ibid., 119.

3. Corrie Ten Boom, *Tramp for the Lord*, (Grand Rapids, Mich.; Fleming H. Revell, 1974), 55–57.

Chapter 8: Healed by the Body

1. I'm not denying there is a place for church discipline as outlined in 1 Corinthians 5, but it is a potent tonic to be used wisely, for it can hurt as well as heal.

Chapter 10: We, the Priests: A High Calling for Lowly People

1. *The Mission*, prod. David Putnam, 125 min., Warner Home Videos, 1986, videocassette.